The Women's Institute

perfect
pies and tarts

Moyra Fraser

First published in Great Britain
by Simon & Schuster UK Ltd, 2011
A CBS Company

Simon & Schuster
Illustrated Books,
Simon & Schuster UK Ltd, 1ˢᵗ Floor,
222 Gray's Inn Road, London WC1X 8HB

1 2 3 4 5 6 7 8 9 10

Editorial Director: **Francine Lawrence**
Commercial Director: **Ami Richards**
Senior Commissioning Editor: **Nicky Hill**
Project Editor: **Nicki Lampon**
Designer: **Fiona Andreanelli**
Photographer: **Myles New**
Stylist: **Rachel Jukes**
Recipe Development and Food Stylist: **Moyra Fraser**
Production Manager: **Katherine Thornton**

Colour reproduction by **Dot Gradations Ltd, UK**

Printed and bound in China

A CIP catalogue for this book is
available from the British Library.

ISBN 978-0-85720-355-7

Notes on the recipes
Both metric and imperial measurements have been
given in all recipes. Use one set of measurements
only and not a mixture of both. Spoon measures are
level and 1 tablespoon = 15 ml, 1 teaspoon = 5 ml.

Preheat ovens before use and cook on the centre
shelf unless cooking more than one item. If using
a fan oven, reduce the heat by 10–20°C, but check
with your handbook.

Medium eggs have been used unless otherwise stated.

This book contains recipes made with nuts.
Those with known allergic reactions to nuts
and nut derivatives, pregnant and breast-
feeding women and very young children
should avoid these dishes.

Contents

Introduction

A beautiful home-made pie or tart is a wonderful thing to make and share, but the idea of making pastry can evoke great angst in some kitchens. Undoubtedly it takes longer than opening a pack, and things can go wrong, but the gratification of producing good home-made pastry is unbeatable, the flavour is superior and it's so much cheaper!

All the basic pastry recipes you will need are here at the beginning of the book, and all are feasible for beginners. Each main recipe will suggest which pastry to use, but do experiment.

Only the most enthusiastic pastry maker will make their own puff pastry, as it does take time and patience, so we have not included a puff pastry recipe as we assume that most people will buy it ready made.

We have given quantities for using chilled, shop-bought pastry too. When buying ready-made pastry (shortcrust or puff), do opt for the chilled, all-butter varieties when possible. They have a much better flavour and any leftovers can be frozen for up to 1 month.

We have also included a recipe for gluten-free pastry using a widely available flour blend. If you don't want to make your own, there are one or two ready-made, frozen, gluten-free pastries available to buy either online or from good supermarkets.

Hints & tips

Hands free

Conventional wisdom has it that cold hands and a light touch are essential for making shortcrust pastry, where fat is rubbed into flour until it forms 'breadcrumbs'. While this is not nearly as tricky as many people suggest, by far the best option is to make the pastry in a food processor, and we suggest this here in our recipes. This keeps handling to a minimum, is very quick and easy and produces a delicious pastry with a crisp texture.

Baking tins

To make life easier, we have kept the number of different baking tins to a minimum. All the large round tarts and flans are made in 23 cm (9 inch) base measurement, loose-based, fluted flan tins, either 2.5 cm (1 inch) or 4.5–5 cm (1¾–2 inches) deep. The individual tartlets are all made in 9 cm (3½ inch) base measurement, loose-based, fluted flan tins, either 2 cm (¾ inch) or 3 cm (1½ inch) deep.

Lining tins

To line a tart tin, remove the pastry from the fridge and turn it out on to a lightly floured surface. Dust a rolling pin with flour and roll the pastry out so that it is slightly larger than your tart tin – about an extra 5 cm (2 inches) in diameter. Rotate the pastry in quarter turns as you roll to produce an even circle that doesn't stick to the work surface. Roll the pastry over the lightly floured rolling pin and unroll over the tin. Press the pastry into the shape of the tin and trim. Prick the base with a fork and chill.

Baking blind

Most of the pastry cases in these recipes do require to be 'baked blind'. This means pre-cooking the pastry-lined tin to give a good crisp crust and avoid soggy-bottomed pies and tarts.

Traditional recipes line the chilled, pastry-lined tart tins with greaseproof paper and ceramic baking beans, but our recipes suggest freezing the tins for 30 minutes to firm the pastry then lining closely with foil. This helps to prevent the pastry from shrinking, conducts the heat to the pastry and gives a neater pastry case. The case takes longer to bake blind but the end result is better. Use ceramic baking beans if you have them, or simply keep a jar of dried pulses such as chick peas or beans to use for the purpose.

When baking blind sweet pastry, the top edges will brown first, so keep the top covered with a ring of foil, if necessary, to protect the edges while the rest of the pastry case continues to cook.

Storing

Uncooked pastry will keep, wrapped in cling film, in the fridge for up to 3 days or for 1 month in the freezer. Baked pastry cases can be wrapped and frozen for up to 3 months. To use, unwrap and thaw at room temperature for about 2 hours. Pop them back in the original tin to continue with your chosen recipe.

Basic pastry recipes

Rich shortcrust pastry

This is a sweet basic shortcrust pastry used for open-faced flans and tarts. It's richer than shortcrust, but very crisp with a shortbread-like texture.

Makes see Tips
Preparation time: 10–15 minutes
+ 30 minutes chilling

175 g (6 oz) **plain white flour**
½ teaspoon **salt**
100 g (3½ oz) chilled **unsalted butter**, diced
1 tablespoon **icing sugar**
1 large **egg yolk**, beaten
2–4 tablespoons chilled **water**

Put the flour, salt, butter and icing sugar in a food processor and whizz for about 10 seconds until the mixture resembles fine breadcrumbs. Use the pulse button to avoid over-working the mixture.

Add the egg yolk and about 2 tablespoons of chilled water and whizz again for 2–3 seconds until the ingredients begin to stick together. Add a further 1–2 tablespoons of chilled water if the mixture still looks dry and crumbly, but the less liquid used the better (see Tips).

Collect the mixture together with lightly floured hands and knead lightly on a floured surface for 20–30 seconds. Shape the dough into a flat disc. Wrap in cling film and chill for 30 minutes before using.

Tips
This quantity will easily line a 23 cm (9 inch) round, 2.5 cm (1 inch) deep, loose-based, fluted flan tin, a 34 x 11.5 cm (13½ x 4½ inch) loose-based tranche tin or six 9 cm (3½ inch) round, 2 cm (¾ inch) deep, loose-based individual fluted tartlet tins.

If using a 4.5–5 cm (1¾–2 inch) deep flan tin or 3 cm (1½ inch) deep individual tartlet tins, make a larger quantity of pastry using 225 g (8 oz) of flour, ½ teaspoon of salt, 150 g (5½ oz) of butter, 1 tablespoon of sugar, 1 medium whole egg and 4–5 tablespoons of water.

Water makes the pastry easier to handle but too much will produce a hard crust that is more likely to shrink in the oven. Exact quantities of liquid are difficult to give as the amount that flour will absorb can vary significantly, so keep adding it in small amounts until the ingredients begin to clump together in the bowl.

Variations
Orange shortcrust: Add the finely grated zest of 1 orange with the egg mixture.

Vanilla shortcrust: Add the seeds from a vanilla pod to the dry ingredients.

Lavender shortcrust: Leave one head of fresh lavender tucked into the icing sugar for 1 hour. Discard the lavender before using the sugar.

Sweet flan pastry

This is the rich, buttery and crisp pastry used for sweet French patisserie. Traditionally the pastry is mixed by hand but this method is much simpler.

Makes see Tips
Preparation time: 10–15 minutes
  + 30 minutes chilling

75 g (2¾ oz) **unsalted butter**, at room temperature
75 g (2¾ oz) **caster sugar**
1 large **egg**, beaten
175 g (6 oz) **plain white flour**
½ teaspoon **salt**
1–2 tablespoons chilled **water**

Place the butter and sugar in a food processor and whizz until just combined. Add the egg and whizz for 30 seconds. Use the pulse button to avoid over-working the pastry.

Tip in the flour and salt and whizz for a few seconds until the ingredients begin to stick together. Add a tablespoon or two of chilled water if the mixture looks dry and crumbly.

Collect the mixture together with lightly floured hands and knead lightly on a floured surface for 20–30 seconds. Shape the dough into a flat disc. Wrap in cling film and chill for 30 minutes before using.

Tips
This quantity will line a 23 cm (9 inch) round, 2.5 cm (1 inch) deep, loose-based, fluted flan tin, a 34 x 11.5 cm (13½ x 4½ inch) loose-based tranche tin or six 9 cm (3½ inch) round, 2 cm (¾ inch) deep, loose-based individual fluted tartlet tins.

If using a 4.5–5 cm (1¾–2 inch) deep flan tin or 2.5 cm (1 inch) deep individual tartlet tins, make a larger quantity of pastry using 125 g (4½ oz) of butter, 125 g (4½ oz) of sugar, 1 large egg plus 1 egg yolk, 225 g (8 oz) of flour and the salt and water.

Sweet flan pastry can often be tricky to roll. Rather than rolling your pastry into a flat sheet, shape it into a short fat sausage. Wrap in cling film and chill for 30 minutes in the fridge. When the pastry is quite firm, cut off thin slices and lay them closely together and slightly overlapping in the tart tin. Push the edges together with your hand, filling in any gaps between the slices to cover the base and sides of the tin. Line with foil and baking beans and bake in the usual way.

Easiest pie pastry

The making of this pastry breaks all the rules but produces a buttery, flaky pastry that's excellent for any double crust pies.

Makes see Tip
Preparation time: 10–15 minutes
  + 1 hour chilling

75 g (2¾ oz) **unsalted butter**, softened
75 g (2¾ oz) **caster sugar**
1 **egg yolk**
grated zest of 1 small **lemon**
125 g (4½ oz) **plain white flour**
½ teaspoon **salt**
¼ teaspoon **baking powder**

Put the butter and sugar in a food processor and whizz together until light and fluffy. Mix in the egg, continue beating and then add the lemon zest.

Sift together the flour, salt and the baking powder, then fold into the butter and sugar mixture.

Shape the dough into a ball with lightly floured hands and place on a floured work surface. Knead very lightly for 20–30 seconds, then wrap in cling film and chill for 1 hour before using.

Tip
This quantity will line a 23 cm (9 inch) round, 4.5–5 cm (1¾–2 inch) deep, loose-based flan tin or six 9 cm (3½ inch) round, 3 cm (1½ inch) deep, loose-based individual fluted tartlet tins.

Chocolate hazelnut crust

A rich, crumbly mixture that can be used in any recipe that uses Sweet flan pastry (see page 9).

Makes see Tips
Preparation time: 10–15 minutes
  + 30 minutes chilling

50 g (1¾ oz) blanched, toasted **hazelnuts**
200 g (7 oz) **plain white flour**
1 tablespoon **cocoa powder**
50 g (1¾ oz) **icing sugar**
½ teaspoon **salt**
125 g (4½ oz) chilled **unsalted butter**, diced
1 large **egg**, beaten

Whizz the hazelnuts in a food processor for a few seconds until finely ground. Add the flour, cocoa powder, sugar and salt and whizz again until blended.

Add the butter and whizz again for a few seconds until the mixture resembles fine breadcrumbs.

Add the egg a little at a time and pulse until the mixture begins to stick together. Remove and knead lightly into a fat sausage shape. Wrap in cling film and chill for 30 minutes before using.

Tips
This quantity will line a 23 cm (9 inch) round, 2.5 cm (1 inch) deep, loose-based, fluted flan tin, a 34 x 11.5 cm (13½ x 4½ inch) loose-based tranche tin or six 9 cm (3½ inch) round, 2 cm (¾ inch) deep, loose-based individual fluted tartlet tins.

To use, slice the chilled pastry thickly and lay the slices in the base of a flan tin, overlapping slightly. Press down, pushing the dough into the base and up the sides. Prick with a fork and freeze for 30 minutes. Preheat the oven to 180°C/350°F/Gas Mark 4. Line the tin with foil and bake blind for 10 minutes. Remove the foil and bake for a further 10 minutes before filling.

Sweet nut pastry

A delicious rich pastry that's perfect for fruit-filled flan cases.

Makes see Tip
Preparation time: 10–15 minutes
+ 30 minutes chilling

100 g (3½ oz) **plain white flour**
50 g (1¾ oz) finely ground **hazelnuts**, **walnuts** or **pecan nuts**
50 g (1¾ oz) **caster sugar**
50 g (1¾ oz) chilled **unsalted butter**, diced
1 **egg**, beaten

Put the flour, nuts and sugar into a food processor and whizz for a few seconds to mix together. Use the pulse button to avoid over-working the pastry.

Add the chilled butter and whizz for about 10 seconds until the mixture resembles fine breadcrumbs. Tip in half the

egg and whizz for a few seconds more until the ingredients begin to stick together, adding a little more egg if the mixture looks dry.

Collect the mixture together with lightly floured hands and knead lightly on a floured surface for 20–30 seconds. Shape the dough into a flat disc. Wrap in cling film and chill for 30 minutes before using.

Tip
This quantity will line a 23 cm (9 inch) round, 4.5–5 cm (1¾–2 inch) deep, loose-based flan tin or six 9 cm (3½ inch) round, 2.5 cm (1 inch) deep, loose-based individual tartlet tins.

Coconut pastry

A crisp pastry that's perfect for any tropical fruit mix.

Makes see Tips
Preparation time: 10–15 minutes
+ 20 minutes chilling

25 g (1 oz) **creamed coconut**
2 tablespoons boiling **water**
175 g (6 oz) **plain white flour**
a pinch of **salt**
100 g (3½ oz) chilled **unsalted butter**, diced
25 g (1 oz) **icing sugar**
a little freshly squeezed **lime juice** or chilled **water**

Dissolve the creamed coconut in the boiling water. Mix to a smooth paste and allow to cool.

Whizz the flour, salt and butter in a food processor until the mixture resembles fine breadcrumbs. Add the icing sugar, creamed coconut paste and 2–3 tablespoons of lime juice or chilled water to bind the mixture together to form a soft dough.

Wrap in cling film and chill in the fridge for about 20 minutes before using.

Tips

This quantity will line a 23 cm (9 inch) round, 2.5 cm (1 inch) deep, loose-based, fluted flan tin, a 34 x 11.5 cm (13½ x 4½ inch) loose-based tranche tin or six 9 cm (3½ inch) round, 2 cm (¾ inch) deep, loose-based individual fluted tartlet tins.

Omit the sugar and use to make spicy savoury tarts and pies.

Soured cream flaky pastry

This buttery, soured cream pastry has a crisp flaky texture and sweetness that's perfect for any pies and flans.

Makes see Tip
Preparation time: 10 minutes
+ 30 minutes chilling

225 g (8 oz) **plain white flour**
25 g (1 oz) **icing sugar**
a pinch of **salt**
175 g (6 oz) chilled **unsalted butter**, diced
6 level tablespoons **soured cream**

Put the flour, icing sugar and salt in a food processor and whizz for a few seconds to combine.

Add the butter and pulse for a few seconds until the mixture resembles fine breadcrumbs. Add the soured cream and pulse again until the mixture begins to stick together.

Knead lightly into a flat disc on a floured surface, wrap in cling film and chill for 30 minutes.

Tip

This quantity will line a 23 cm (9 inch) round, 4.5–5 cm (1¾–2 inch) deep, loose-based flan tin or six 9 cm (3½ inch) round, 3cm (1½in) deep, loose-based, individual tartlet tins.

Variation

Flavour the pastry with 1 teaspoon of ground cinnamon or add the grated zest of 1 orange.

Gluten-free shortcrust pastry

Use this pastry in any of the recipes that require a shortcrust or sweet flan pastry.

Makes see Tips
Preparation time: 10 minutes
+ 30 minutes chilling

200 g (7 oz) **Doves gluten-free plain white flour**
½ teaspoon **salt**
100 g (3½ oz) chilled **unsalted butter**, diced
4 tablespoons chilled **water**

Put the flour, salt and butter in a food processor and whizz for about 10 seconds until the mixture resembles fine breadcrumbs. Use the pulse button to avoid over-working the mixture.

Add the chilled water and whizz again for 2–3 seconds until the ingredients begin to stick together.

Collect the mixture together with lightly floured hands and knead lightly for 20–30 seconds on a floured surface. Shape the dough into a flat disc. Wrap in cling film and rest in the fridge for 30 minutes before using.

Tips
This quantity will line a 23 cm (9 inch) round, 2.5 cm (1 inch) deep, loose-based, fluted flan tin, a 34 x 11.5 cm (13½ x 4½ inch) loose-based tranche tin or six 9 cm (3½ inch) round, 2 cm (¾ inch) deep, loose-based individual fluted tartlet tins.

The pastry dough will appear quite wet at first but does absorb the liquid after the resting time.

To use, roll the pastry out on a lightly floured surface between two pieces of cling film or on a non-stick pastry mat. Line your baking tin and bake blind (see page 6). If the pastry cracks while lining the tin, just patch it up with a little extra pastry. Once cooked, brush the inside of the pastry very lightly with beaten egg and return to the oven for 2–3 minutes. Continue with fillings as in the recipe.

The absence of gluten makes this pastry quite crumbly, but brushing the cooked pastry case lightly with beaten egg seals up any cracks and strengthens the crust.

Ready-made, gluten-free pastries are also available from major supermarkets and online.

French apple flan

This version of the traditional French dish has a delicious, crisp base and a filling of nut cream, topped with apple purée and glazed apple slices.

Serves 6–8
Preparation time:
45 minutes +
30 minutes chilling +
cooling
Cooking time:
60–65 minutes

225 g (8 oz) chilled **puff pastry**
4 small **eating apples**
juice of 1 **lemon**
15 g (½ oz) **butter**, melted
2 tablespoons **demerara sugar**
5 tablespoons smooth **apricot jam**
2 tablespoons boiling **water**

Filling
50 g (1¾ oz) **butter**, softened
50 g (1¾ oz) **caster sugar**
1 large **egg**, beaten
50 g (1¾ oz) **ground hazelnuts** or **almonds**

Apple purée
450 g (1 lb) **cooking apples**
25 g (1 oz) **butter**
2 tablespoons **caster sugar**

Roll out the pastry on a lightly floured surface to about 3 mm (⅛ inch) thick and use to line a 23 cm (9 inch), loose-based, fluted flan tin, about 2.5 cm (1 inch) deep. Prick the base all over with a fork and then freeze for 30 minutes. Preheat the oven to 220°C/425°F/Gas Mark 7.

To make the filling, cream together the butter and sugar until light and fluffy. Add the egg a little at a time. Fold in the ground nuts, cover and chill until firm – about 30 minutes.

For the purée, peel, core and chop the apples, then place in a small saucepan and add the butter and sugar. Cover and cook until the apples are softened (about 10–15 minutes). Cool, cover and chill until needed.

Line the frozen pastry case with a sheet of foil, pressing it gently into the curves of the tin and folding it down carefully over the outside. Fill with baking beans and bake in the preheated oven for 15 minutes.

Remove the foil and beans, prick the pastry base again, then bake for a further 10–15 minutes or until the pastry is golden. If necessary, use a little beaten egg to brush over any cracks and return to the oven for 2–3 minutes to seal. Cool. Reduce the oven temperature to 190°C/375°F/Gas Mark 5.

Peel, core and thinly slice the apples, then toss in the lemon juice to prevent them from discolouring. Spread the filling over the base of the cool flan and top with the apple purée. Arrange the apple slices over the flan, brush with melted butter and sprinkle over the demerara sugar.

Bake the flan for about 35 minutes or until the filling is lightly set and the apples are golden brown at the edges. Cool in the tin for about 30 minutes, then ease out and place on a serving plate. Heat the apricot jam with the boiling water and brush all over the flan. Serve warm or cold.

Variation Drop a star anise into the simmering cooking apples for a subtly fragrant flavour. Remove before using the apple purée.

Tarte au citron

In the 1980s, the Roux brothers' Tarte au Citron caught the public's imagination.
Use a 375 g pack of ready-made chilled shortcrust pastry if you wish.

Serves 6–8
Preparation time:
 35 minutes +
 30 minutes chilling +
 overnight chilling
Cooking time:
 55–65 minutes

1 quantity **Rich shortcrust
 pastry** (see page 8)

Filling
150 g (5½ oz) **caster sugar**
4 **eggs**, plus 1 **egg yolk**,
 beaten
200 ml (7 fl oz) **double cream**
strained juice of 4 large
 lemons (about 125 ml/
 4½ fl oz)
1 tablespoon finely grated
 lemon zest
icing sugar, for dusting

Put a baking sheet in the oven and preheat to 200°C/400°F/Gas Mark 6. Roll out the pastry on a lightly floured surface to about 3 mm (⅛ inch) thick, then use it to line a 23 cm (9 inch) loose-based, fluted flan tin, about 2.5 cm (1 inch) deep. Prick the base with a fork and pop it in the freezer for 30 minutes.

Line the frozen pastry case with a sheet of foil, pressing it gently into the curves of the tin and folding it down carefully over the outside. Fill with baking beans and bake on the baking sheet for 15 minutes.

Remove the foil and beans and bake for a further 5–10 minutes or until the pastry is firm and pale golden brown round the edges. If necessary, use a little of the beaten egg to brush over any cracks and return to the oven for 2–3 minutes to seal. Reduce the oven temperature to 140°C/275°F/Gas Mark 1.

Whisk together the sugar and eggs until the sugar has completely dissolved. Lightly whip the cream until it just begins to hold its shape and fold in. Gradually stir in the lemon juice and zest.

Pour the mixture into the pastry case and bake for 35–40 minutes until lightly set but still wobbly in the centre. Leave to cool then refrigerate overnight. Serve chilled, dusted with icing sugar.

Tips Once the tart is in the oven and level, spoon in a little extra filling to bring it right up to the pastry edge.

The most important thing to remember is to remove the tart from the oven when it's still wobbly in the middle.

Grating lemon zest is so much easier with a super-sharp microplane grater. They are expensive, but well worth it if you bake regularly.

Variation Put the finished tart under a hot grill for 1–2 minutes or use a cook's blowtorch to caramelise the icing sugar. Chill again for 30 minutes before serving.

Bakewell tart

This recipe revives one of our most famous tarts in its original glory; ideal for fairs and coffee mornings. Use 1½ x 375 g packs of ready-made chilled dessert pastry if you wish.

Serves 8–10
Preparation time:
  30 minutes +
  30 minutes chilling +
  cooling
Cooking time:
  50–65 minutes

1 large quantity **Sweet flan pastry** (see Tip, page 9)
250 g (9 oz) **unsalted butter**, at room temperature
200 g (7 oz) **caster sugar**
3 **eggs**, lightly beaten
1 teaspoon **vanilla extract**
250 g (9 oz) **ground almonds**
3 tablespoons **plain white flour**
4 tablespoons good quality **strawberry conserve**
3 tablespoons smooth **apricot conserve**
2 tablespoons boiling **water**

Put a baking sheet in the oven and preheat to 200°C/400°F/Gas Mark 6. Roll out the pastry on a lightly floured surface to about 3 mm (⅛ inch) thick, then use it to line a 23 cm (9 inch) loose-based, fluted flan tin, about 4.5–5 cm (1¾–2 inches) deep. Prick the base with a fork and pop in the freezer for 30 minutes. Re-roll the pastry trimmings to a rough rectangle, place on a baking sheet and chill for 30 minutes.

Line the frozen pastry case with a sheet of foil, pressing it gently into the curves of the tin and folding it down carefully over the outside. Fill with baking beans and bake on the baking sheet for 15 minutes.

Remove the foil and beans, then bake for a further 5–10 minutes or until the pastry is firm and pale golden brown around the edges. If necessary, use a little beaten egg to brush over any cracks and return to the oven for 2–3 minutes to seal. Reduce the oven temperature to 180°C/350°F/Gas Mark 4.

Beat together the butter and sugar until light and fluffy. Gradually beat in the eggs and vanilla extract, then fold in the ground almonds and flour. Spread a thin layer of strawberry conserve over the base of the pastry case then spoon in the almond mixture and spread evenly.

Cut the chilled rectangle of pastry into long, finger-wide strips. Use these to create a lattice pattern on top of the filling, leaving roughly 2.5 cm (1 inch) between them. Bake for 30–40 minutes until the top is a pale golden brown. Leave to cool a little.

Heat the apricot conserve with the boiling water and brush over the top of the warm tart. Cool completely before serving.

Tip The best bakewell tarts are made with home-made conserve, so if you opt for shop-bought, use a good quality conserve or a reduced sugar variety so that the finished tart will not be too sweet.

Variation Use any good quality conserve such as black cherry to spread over the base of the pastry case.

Maids of honour

These little curd tarts are believed to have originated in the royal kitchens at Hampton Court Palace.

Makes 12
Preparation time:
30 minutes + cooling
Cooking time:
25–30 minutes

1 quantity **Soured cream flaky pastry** (see page 12)
25 g (1 oz) **butter**, softened
50 g (1¾ oz) **curd cheese**
1 **egg**
2 teaspoons **lemon juice**
1 tablespoon **brandy**
25 g (1 oz) **caster sugar**
1 tablespoon **ground almonds**
a pinch of grated **nutmeg**, plus extra for dusting
grated zest of 1 **lemon**
icing sugar, for dusting

Put a baking sheet in the oven and preheat to 190°C/375°F/Gas Mark 5. Roll the pastry out on a lightly floured surface to about 3 mm (⅛ inch) thick. Using a 7.5 cm (3 inch) round cutter, stamp out 12 rounds and use to line a 12-hole shallow bun tin. Chill until needed.

Beat together the butter, curd cheese, egg, lemon juice and brandy until thoroughly combined. Whisk in the sugar, almonds, nutmeg and lemon zest. Divide the curd cheese mixture between the tartlets, filling them almost to the top.

Bake the tartlets on the baking sheet for 25–30 minutes or until just set and golden. Cool in the tins for about 5 minutes then ease out. Eat warm or cold within 1 day, dusted with icing sugar and a little extra nutmeg.

Tips When stamping out the pastry, don't be tempted to twist the cutter but lift it straight off. This way, the pastry will rise more evenly.

If you can't find curd cheese, use sieved full fat cottage cheese instead.

Variation Omit the lemon juice and brandy and use orange juice with Cointreau.

Tarte des demoiselles tatin

This is an upside-down caramelised apple tart from the Lamotte-Beuvron region of France. Serve with crème fraîche.

Serves 6–8
Preparation time:
45 minutes +
45 minutes chilling
Cooking time:
20 minutes

Pastry
225 g (8 oz) **plain white flour**
½ teaspoon **salt**
50 g (1¾ oz) **caster sugar**
125 g (4½ oz) chilled
   unsalted butter, diced
½ teaspoon **vanilla extract**
3 tablespoons **crème
   fraîche**
6 tablespoons chilled **water**

Filling
8 **Golden Delicious apples**
   (about 900 g/2 lb)
juice of 1 **lemon**
75 g (2¾ oz) **butter**, softened
125 g (4½ oz) **caster sugar**

For the pastry, mix the flour, salt and sugar together in a bowl, add the butter and stir in with the vanilla extract, crème fraîche and chilled water. Stir gently. The dough will be very crumbly but bring together with one hand (don't knead), wrap in cling film and chill for about 45 minutes.

For the filling, peel, core and quarter the apples and toss in the lemon juice to prevent discolouring. Spread the butter over the base of a 23 cm (9 inch) moule a manqué tin, round flameproof dish or ovenproof frying pan and sprinkle over the caster sugar. Pack the apples, rounded side down, almost overlapping to cover the bottom completely.

Place the dish directly over a moderate to high heat for about 15 minutes, or until the sugar and butter begin to bubble and caramelise. Watch that the apples don't burn and that the sugar caramelises evenly. Preheat the oven to 200°C/400°F/Gas Mark 6.

Roll out the pastry to the size of the tin. Place it over the caramelised apples, tucking in any rough edges. Stand the tin on a baking sheet and bake for 20 minutes.

Put a plate over the tart and carefully invert (there will be liquid caramel underneath). The apples should be sticky, the pastry crisp.

Tips There's no need for a special tin, anything round, shallow and ovenproof will work well.

It will look as though there is too much butter when caramelising the apples but the mixture gradually blends together.

Variations Use cinnamon-flavoured sugar when caramelising the apples for a mild spicy flavour.

Replace the apples with ripe but firm pears.

Treacle tart

This old favourite demonstrates how the simplest ingredients can be transformed into a heavenly pudding. Use a 375 g pack of ready-made chilled shortcrust pastry if you wish.

Serves 6–8
Preparation time:
  25 minutes +
  30 minutes chilling +
  cooling
Cooking time:
  55–70 minutes

1 quantity **Rich shortcrust pastry** (see page 8)
475 g (1 lb 1 oz) **golden syrup**
125 g (4½ oz) fresh **white breadcrumbs**
finely grated zest of 2 **lemons**
2 **eggs**, beaten
ice cream or **custard**, to serve

Put a baking sheet in the oven and preheat to 200°C/400°F/Gas Mark 6. Roll out the pastry on a lightly floured surface to about 3 mm (⅛ inch) thick, then use it to line a 23 cm (9 inch) loose-based, fluted flan tin, about 2.5 cm (1 inch) deep. Prick the base with a fork and pop in the freezer for 30 minutes.

Line the frozen pastry case with a sheet of foil, pressing it gently into the curves of the tin and folding it down carefully over the outside. Fill with baking beans and bake on the baking sheet for 15 minutes.

Remove the foil and beans, then bake for a further 5–10 minutes or until the pastry is firm and pale golden brown around the edges. If necessary, use a little beaten egg to brush over any cracks and return to the oven for 2–3 minutes to seal. Reduce the oven temperature to 180°C/350°F/Gas Mark 4.

Meanwhile gently warm the golden syrup in a saucepan for 2–3 minutes. Remove from the heat and stir in the breadcrumbs and lemon zest. Stir the beaten eggs into the syrup mixture, and then pour the filling into the pastry case.

Bake for about 35–45 minutes or until the filling is lightly set and golden brown. Allow to cool slightly then serve warm with ice cream or custard.

Tip When making fresh breadcrumbs, it's best to use bread that is 1 or 2 days old.

Variations Use 400 g (14 oz) of golden syrup mixed with 75 g (2¾ oz) of maple syrup for a delicious rich nutty flavour.

Omit the lemon zest and use the grated zest of 1 large orange instead.

Egg custard tartlets

These delicious, deep tartlets are perfect on their own or with a fruit compote. Use a 500 g pack of ready-made chilled shortcrust pastry if you wish.

Makes 6
Preparation time:
20 minutes +
30 minutes chilling +
cooling
Cooking time:
45–55 minutes

1 large quantity **Rich shortcrust pastry** (see Tip, page 8)
2 **eggs**, beaten
100 ml (3½ fl oz) full-fat **crème fraîche** or **double cream**
100 ml (3½ fl oz) **single cream**
50 g (1¾ oz) **caster sugar**
½ teaspoon **mixed spice** or **ground cinnamon**
2–3 drops **vanilla extract**
icing sugar and **nutmeg**, for dusting

Put a baking sheet in the oven and preheat to 200°C/400°F/Gas Mark 6. Roll out the pastry on a lightly floured surface to about 3 mm (⅛ inch) thick, then use it to line a six-hole, deep muffin tin or Yorkshire pudding tins. There is no need to be too neat with the edges. Prick the pastry with a fork and pop in the freezer for 30 minutes.

Line each pastry case with a small sheet of foil, pressing it gently into the sides and folding it down carefully over the top edge of the pastry. Fill the cases with baking beans and bake on the baking sheet for 10 minutes.

Remove the foil and beans, then bake for a further 5–10 minutes or until the pastry is firm and golden brown. If necessary, use a little beaten egg to brush over any cracks and return to the oven for 2–3 minutes to seal. Reduce the oven temperature to 170°C/320°F/Gas Mark 3.

Whisk together the remaining ingredients and strain into the pastry cases. Bake for 30–35 minutes or until the custard is very lightly set but still quite wobbly in the centre. Leave to cool, then chill in the tins. Serve reheated or chilled, dusted with a little icing sugar and nutmeg.

Tips Any deep, individual tins can be used, but they should have a capacity of about 150 ml (5 fl oz).

The cooked tartlets can be made a day ahead, kept in the fridge and warmed through in a low oven (170°C/320°F/Gas Mark 3) for 10 minutes before serving.

Using a mix of crème fraîche and cream produces a custard that is a little less rich; you could use all cream if you like.

Variations Add 1 tablespoon of finely chopped stem ginger to the custard mixture or flavour the custard with the finely grated zest of 1 small orange.

Croustade aux pommes

This exquisite pudding from the south of France is the perfect way to end a meal. Serve with crème fraîche or crème anglaise custard.

Serves 6–8
Preparation time:
  30 minutes + cooling
Cooking time:
  45 minutes

50 g (1¾ oz) **walnut pieces**
175 g (6 oz) **no-soak pitted prunes**, roughly chopped
2 tablespoons **Armagnac** or other **brandy**
125 g (4½ oz) **butter**
75 g (2¾ oz) **caster sugar**
finely grated zest and juice of 1 **lemon**
1 large **egg**
25 g (1 oz) **self-raising flour**
½ teaspoon **ground cinnamon**
450 g (1 lb) crisp **eating apples**, peeled, cored and sliced
270 g pack chilled **filo pastry**

Put a baking sheet in the oven and preheat to 190°C/375°F/Gas Mark 5.

Place the walnuts on a second baking tray and toast in the hot oven or under the grill. Cool, and then finely chop. Put the prunes in a bowl and add the Armagnac. Set aside.

Beat together 50 g (1¾ oz) of the butter with 50 g (1¾ oz) of the sugar, the lemon zest, egg, flour, ¼ level teaspoon cinnamon and the walnuts. Mix the apples with the remaining sugar and cinnamon and 1 tablespoon of lemon juice.

Melt the remaining butter and lightly grease a 23 cm (9 inch) loose-based, fluted flan tin, 2.5 cm (1 inch) deep. Use about three-quarters of the pastry to line the tin, brushing lightly with butter after each layer and allowing about 7.5 cm (3 inches) of pastry to hang over the sides of the tin.

Spread the walnut mixture over the pastry base and top with the apples and then the soaked prunes. Fold the pastry edges over the filling and top with two more buttered pastry layers. Crumple up any remaining pastry and scatter over the pie. Drizzle with the remaining melted butter.

Bake on the baking sheet for about 45 minutes, covering loosely with foil when well browned. Cool for about 20 minutes then serve warm.

Tips The croustade can be made the day before needed and warmed through in a moderate (180°C/350°F/Gas Mark 4) oven before serving.

It is easier to cut prunes with scissors than a chopping knife.

Variation Substitute ripe rosy pears for the apples.

Brandy butter mince pies

A little brandy butter in the base of each of these melt-in-the-mouth mince pies gives a surprising 'kick'. Use a 375 g pack of ready-made chilled shortcrust pastry if you wish.

Makes around 12
Preparation time:
 30 minutes +
 30 minutes chilling +
 cooling
Cooking time:
 20–25 minutes

1 quantity **Rich shortcrust pastry** (see page 8)

Filling
25 g (1 oz) **unsalted butter**, softened
25 g (1 oz) **light soft brown sugar**
1 teaspoon **brandy**
finely grated zest of ½ **orange**
about 225 g (8 oz) home-made **mincemeat** (see Tips)
1 **egg**, beaten, to glaze

For the filling, beat together the butter and soft brown sugar until pale and creamy. Gradually beat in the brandy and orange zest. Chill for 30 minutes until firm.

Preheat the oven to 200°C/400°F/Gas Mark 6. Cut off about half of the pastry and set aside. Roll out the remainder on a lightly floured surface to just under 3 mm (⅛ inch) thick and stamp out 12 rounds with an 8 cm (3¼ inch) round fluted cutter, re-rolling the trimmings as necessary. Use the pastry rounds to line a 12-hole shallow bun tin. Put a knob of the chilled brandy butter into each pastry case and top each with 2 teaspoons of mincemeat. Brush the pastry edge with a little beaten egg.

Roll out the reserved pastry a little thinner and stamp out 12 rounds with a 6.5 cm (2½ inch) round cutter. Put on top of the mincemeat and press down to seal. Brush with a little more egg and bake for 20–25 minutes until golden. Cool a little before serving.

Tips The uncooked mince pies will freeze well in their tins. Cover tightly with cling film and freeze for up to 1 month. Cook the pies from frozen for 25–30 minutes until golden.

If you don't have a shallow bun tin, the pies can be made flat on a baking sheet.

If using shop-bought mincemeat, use a good quality one. Cheaper varieties tend to be too 'wet'.

Variations Top the pies with star-shaped pieces of white almond marzipan, toasted under the grill, or some traditional crumble mixture before baking.

The pies can also be topped with swirls of meringue mixture, but reduce the oven temperature to 180°C/350°F/Gas Mark 4 and bake for 35–40 minutes or simply brown under a hot grill after baking for the usual time.

Lemon meringue pie

Serves 6–8
Preparation time:
  60 minutes +
  30 minutes chilling
Cooking time:
  50–60 minutes

1 quantity **Rich shortcrust pastry** (see page 8) or 375 g pack chilled **shortcrust pastry**

Filling
2 level tablespoons **cornflour**
100 g (3½ oz) **golden caster sugar**
finely grated zest of 2 large **lemons**
juice of 1 small **orange**
juice of 3–4 **lemons** (about 150 ml/5 fl oz)
75 g (2¾ oz) chilled **butter**, diced
3 **egg yolks** and 1 whole **egg**, beaten

Meringue
150 g (5½ oz) **egg whites** (about 5)
1 teaspoon **distilled malt vinegar**
1 level teaspoon **cornflour**
275 g (9½ oz) **icing sugar**

Put a baking sheet in the oven and preheat to 200°C/400°F/Gas Mark 6. Roll out the pastry on a lightly floured surface to about 3 mm (⅛ inch) thick, then use it to line a 23 cm (9 inch) loose-based, fluted flan tin, about 2.5 cm (1 inch) deep. Prick the base with a fork and freeze for 30 minutes.

Line the pastry case with a sheet of foil, pressing it gently into the curves of the tin and folding it down carefully over the outside. Fill with baking beans and bake on the baking sheet for 15 minutes.

Remove the foil and beans, then bake for a further 5–10 minutes or until the pastry is firm and pale golden brown around the edges. If necessary, use a little beaten egg to brush over any cracks and return to the oven for 2–3 minutes to seal. Reduce the oven temperature to 150°C/300°F/Gas Mark 2.

For the filling, mix together the cornflour, sugar and lemon zest in a medium saucepan. Put the orange juice into a measuring jug and make up to 175 ml (6 fl oz) with cold water. Strain in the lemon juice. Gradually stir the juice mixture into the saucepan, stirring all the time.

Cook over a medium heat, stirring constantly, until the sauce thickens to a smooth 'custard'. Once the mixture bubbles, remove from the heat and stir in the butter until melted.

Stir the beaten eggs into the pan and return to a medium heat. Stir vigorously for a few minutes until the mixture thickens and bubbles a couple of times. Remove from the heat.

For the meringue, put the egg whites, vinegar, cornflour and icing sugar in a bowl over a pan of barely simmering water. With an electric whisk, whisk for 10 minutes until very thick and shiny. Off the heat, whisk on the lowest setting for 5–10 minutes or until the bowl feels cool.

Reheat the filling and pour into the pastry case (keeping the case in the tin). Pile the meringue on top of the warm filling, starting at the edge and working into the centre. Make sure there are no gaps.

Cook for a good 30–35 minutes until the meringue is crisp and slightly coloured but soft and mallowy underneath. Let the pie sit in the tin for 20 minutes, then remove and leave for another 20 minutes before slicing. Eat the same day.

Tips For a darker topping, use a cook's blowtorch to turn the peaks golden.

Making a 'cooked meringue' (i.e. whisking all the ingredients together over heat) makes a more stable mixture.

Pecan pies

This New England classic is often disappointingly dry. This version is moist, rich and very more-ish. Use a 500 g pack of ready-made chilled shortcrust pastry if you wish.

Serves 6
Preparation time:
  30 minutes +
  30 minutes chilling
Cooking time:
  35–45 minutes

1 large quantity **Rich shortcrust pastry** (see Tip, page 8)

Filling
2 large **eggs**, beaten
75 g (2¾ oz) **soft dark brown sugar**
125 g (4½ oz) **golden syrup**
25 g (1 oz) **butter**, melted
1 tablespoon **rum**
100 g (3½ oz) **pecan nuts**, half toasted and roughly chopped and half left whole

Put a baking sheet in the oven and preheat to 200°C/400°F/Gas Mark 6. Roll out the pastry on a lightly floured surface to about 3 mm (⅛ inch) thick, then use it to line six 9 cm (3½ inch) round, 2.5 cm (1 inch) deep, loose-based individual tartlet tins. Prick the bases with a fork and pop in the freezer for 30 minutes.

Line each pastry case with a small sheet of foil, pressing it gently into the curves of the tin and folding it down carefully over the outside. Fill with baking beans and bake on the baking sheet for 10 minutes.

Remove the foil and beans, then bake for a further 5–10 minutes or until the pastry is firm and golden brown. If necessary, use a little beaten egg to brush over any cracks and return to the oven for 2–3 minutes to seal. Reduce the oven temperature to 180°C/350°F/Gas Mark 4.

Meanwhile, whisk the eggs until foamy. Add the sugar, golden syrup, butter and rum.

Sprinkle the chopped nuts over the base of the pastry cases and spoon in the filling mixture almost to the top. Sprinkle the whole nuts on top and put the pies back in the oven for about 20–25 minutes. The filling will have puffed up and cracked but don't worry as this will subside on cooling. Serve warm.

Tips Reroll the pastry trimmings and stamp out 18–20 leaf shapes with a small cutter. Place on a baking sheet and chill for 30 minutes. Bake alongside the pies for 7–10 minutes or until golden. Scatter over the pies before serving.

The filling gets stickier if the pies are made a day before needed. Warm them through in a moderate oven (180°C/350°F/Gas Mark 4) for 10 minutes before serving.

Banoffee pie

This version doesn't require boiling the can of condensed milk, as some cans have been known to explode! Use a 500 g pack of ready-made chilled shortcrust pastry if you wish.

Serves 8–10
Preparation time:
  40 minutes +
  75 minutes chilling +
  cooling
Cooking time:
  25 minutes

1 large quantity **Rich
  shortcrust pastry** (see Tip,
  page 8)
175 g (6 oz) **butter**
125 g (4½ oz) **light soft
  brown sugar**
4 tablespoons **milk**
397 g can **condensed milk**
4 **bananas**
½ teaspoon **instant coffee
  granules**
1 teaspoon boiling **water**
300 ml (10 fl oz) **double
  cream**
cocoa powder, for dusting

Put a baking sheet in the oven and preheat to 200°C/400°F/Gas Mark 6. Roll out the pastry on a lightly floured surface to about 3 mm (⅛ inch) thick, then use it to line a 23 cm (9 inch) loose-based, fluted flan tin, about 4.5–5 cm (1¾–2 inches) deep. Prick the base with a fork and pop in the freezer for 30 minutes.

Line the pastry case with a sheet of foil, pressing it gently into the curves of the tin and folding it down carefully over the outside. Fill with baking beans and bake on the baking sheet for 15 minutes.

Remove the foil and beans, then bake for a further 10 minutes or until the pastry is completely cooked, firm and golden brown. If necessary, use a little beaten egg to brush over any cracks and return to the oven for 2–3 minutes to seal.

Meanwhile, place the butter and sugar in a small, heavy-based, non-stick saucepan. Heat gently until the butter melts and the sugar dissolves. Bring to the boil and bubble for 1 minute only, stirring frequently.

Off the heat, add the milk and condensed milk, bring to the boil and bubble for 2 minutes only or until the mixture thickens to the consistency of a very thick sauce and turns golden. Stir constantly or the mixture will burn. Keep warm.

Thickly slice the bananas into the cooked pastry case. Spoon the warm toffee evenly over the fruit and spread to cover completely. Leave to cool, then chill until set, about 45 minutes.

Blend the coffee and boiling water and leave to cool. Whip the cream until it just holds its shape and whisk in the coffee. Spoon the cream roughly over the set toffee filling and return to the fridge. The pie will keep in the fridge for 2–3 hours. Dust a little cocoa powder over the cream before serving.

Tip If the caramel sauce does catch a little while cooking, don't worry. Just sieve the sauce into the pastry case to remove any specks of burnt caramel. It will still taste delicious.

Variations Pour the warm toffee over ripe, peeled, cored and sliced pears, cooked apple or thinly sliced pineapple and mango.

Strawberry tart

A summer favourite when sweet British strawberries are at their very best. Use a 375 g pack of ready-made chilled dessert pastry if you wish.

Serves 6–8
Preparation time:
   35 minutes +
   30 minutes chilling +
   cooling
Cooking time:
   17–25 minutes

1 quantity **Sweet flan pastry**
   (see page 9)

Filling
140 ml (5 fl oz) **double cream**
2 teaspoons **icing sugar**
75 g (2¾ oz) **mascarpone**
400 g (14 oz) small fresh
   strawberries, hulled and
   halved
about 12 large **blueberries**
   (optional)
2 **passion fruit**
about 150 g (5½ oz)
   redcurrant jelly

Put a baking sheet in the oven and preheat to 200°C/400°F/Gas Mark 6. Roll out the pastry on a lightly floured surface to about 3 mm (⅛ inch) thick, then use it to line a 34 x 11.5 cm (13½ x 4½ inch) loose-based tranche tin. Prick the base with a fork and pop in the freezer for 30 minutes.

Line the pastry case with a sheet of foil, pressing it gently into the curves of the tin and folding it down carefully over the outside. Fill the case with baking beans and bake on the baking sheet for 12–15 minutes.

Remove the foil and beans and bake for a further 5–10 minutes, or until completely dried out and golden brown. If necessary, use a little beaten egg to brush over any cracks and return to the oven for 2–3 minutes to seal. Leave to cool in the tin.

Lightly whip the cream with the icing sugar and gradually fold it into the mascarpone until smooth. Spoon into the pastry case. Pile the strawberries on top of the cream with the blueberries, if using.

Halve the passion fruit, scoop out the pulp and sieve to extract the juice. Warm the redcurrant jelly with the passion fruit juice, stirring until smooth. Bring to the boil and brush the hot jelly over the fruit. Keep in a cool place until needed.

Tip Serve the tart within 3 hours of completion or the creamy filling will soften the pastry too much.

Variation Any mixture of berries can be used, e.g. raspberries, strawberries and blueberries. Just keep the total weight the same.

Baklava

This is a traditional Middle Eastern sweet pastry made up of layers of filo pastry brushed with melted butter and sweetened chopped nuts.

Makes 16
Preparation time:
  30 minutes + chilling
  + soaking
Cooking time:
  25–30 minutes

200 g (7 oz) blanched
  almonds
200 g (7 oz) shelled,
  unsalted **pistachio nuts**
3 tablespoons **caster sugar**
200 g (7 oz) **butter**, melted
1½ x 270 g packs chilled **filo**
  pastry

Syrup
175 g (6 oz) **clear honey**
pared zest and juice
  of ½ **lemon**
1 **cinnamon stick**

Put all the syrup ingredients in a saucepan with 200 ml (7 fl oz) of water and bring slowly to the boil. Bubble gently for 7–10 minutes until reduced and syrupy, then leave to cool. Strain into a jug and chill.

Put the almonds and pistachio nuts in a food processor with the sugar and whizz for a few seconds until roughly chopped.

Lightly grease a 30 x 20 cm (12 x 8 inch) Swiss roll tin with a little of the melted butter. Unroll the filo pastry and cover with a clean tea towel.

Preheat the oven to 200°C/400°F/Gas Mark 6. Layer five sheets of pastry over the base of the tin, brushing lightly with butter between each layer. Sprinkle with about one-third of the nut mixture. Top with three more layers of buttered pastry then sprinkle with half the remaining nut mixture. Add three further layers of buttered pastry and sprinkle over the remaining nuts. Finish with five layers of buttered filo pastry and mark the pastry in diagonal lines to make about 16 diamond shapes.

Put the baklava in the oven and reduce the temperature to 180°C/350°F/Gas Mark 4. Bake for 25–30 minutes or until golden brown.

When the Baklava is cooked, cut through the diagonal lines and pour the chilled syrup over the hot pastry. Set aside to soak for at least 2 hours, preferably overnight.

Tip Any leftover filo pastry can be kept, well-wrapped, in the fridge for 2–3 days or frozen for up to 1 month.

Variations Try a few drops
of rosewater in the syrup to replace the cinnamon.

Any combination of nuts can be used; try walnuts, pecans or hazelnuts. Just keep the weight the same.

Warm pine nut tart

A traditional Tuscan recipe that's perfect with vanilla ice cream or cold with coffee. Use 1½ x 375 g packs of ready-made chilled dessert pastry if you wish.

Serves 6–8
Preparation time:
 25 minutes +
 30 minutes chilling +
 cooling
Cooking time:
 50–65 minutes

1 large quantity **Sweet flan pastry** (see Tip, page 9)
50 g (1¾ oz) **butter**
150 g (5½ oz) **light soft brown sugar**
75 ml (3 fl oz) runny, clear **honey**
25 ml (1 fl oz) **golden syrup**
2 large **eggs**, beaten
100 ml (3½ fl oz) **double cream**
50 g (1¾ oz) **pine nuts**
50 g (1¾oz) **plain flour**

Put a baking sheet in the oven and preheat to 200°C/400°F/Gas Mark 6. Roll out the pastry on a lightly floured surface to about 3 mm (⅛ inch) thick, then use it to line a 23 cm (9 inch) loose-based, fluted flan tin, about 4.5–5 cm (1¾–2 inches) deep. Prick the base with a fork and pop in the freezer for 30 minutes.

Line the pastry case with a sheet of foil, pressing it gently into the curves of the tin and folding it down carefully over the outside. Fill with baking beans and bake on the baking sheet for 15 minutes.

Remove the foil and beans, reduce the oven temperature to 180°C/350°F/Gas Mark 4, then bake for a further 5–10 minutes or until the pastry is firm and pale golden brown round the edges. If necessary, use a little beaten egg to brush over any cracks and return to the oven for 2–3 minutes to seal.

Melt 25 g (1 oz) of the butter and whisk together with 125 g (4½ oz) of the soft brown sugar, the honey, syrup, eggs and cream. Pour into the pastry case and bake on the baking sheet for 20–25 minutes or until puffed and golden.

Meanwhile, put the pine nuts, remaining butter and sugar and the flour in a food processor and whizz to a rough crumble texture. Sprinkle over the hot tart and return to the oven for 10–15 minutes until pale golden. Allow to cool slightly, then turn out and serve warm.

Tip This tart is wonderful served with this quick yogurt ice cream: whisk 4 large egg yolks with 125 g (4½ oz) of icing sugar until thick. Fold in 150 ml (5 fl oz) of lightly whipped double cream and 300 ml (10 fl oz) of Greek yogurt. Freeze until firm and use within 24 hours.

Deep-dish apple pie

Make one large pie for Sunday lunch or divide the mixture and make two smaller pies – one for the freezer. Use a 500 g pack of ready-made chilled shortcrust pastry if you wish.

Serves 6
Preparation time:
 35 minutes +
 30 minutes chilling +
 cooling
Cooking time:
 55–60 minutes

1 large quantity **Rich shortcrust pastry** (see Tip, page 8)
900 g (2 lb) **cooking apples**, peeled, cored and thickly sliced
3 **cloves** or 1 **star anise**
50 g (1¾ oz) **butter**
1 teaspoon **mixed spice**
1 **cinnamon stick**
75 g (2¾ oz) **caster sugar**, plus extra for dusting
450 g (1 lb) **dessert apples**, peeled, cored and thickly sliced
1 small **egg**, beaten
demerara sugar, for dusting

Put a baking sheet in the oven and preheat to 200°C/400°F/Gas Mark 6.

Roll out the pastry on a lightly floured surface to about 3 mm (⅛ inch) thick, then use it to line two 15 cm (6 inch) loose-based, fluted flan tins, about 3.75 cm (1½ inches) deep, or one 23 cm (9 inch) loose-based, fluted flan tin, about 4.5–5 cm (1¾–2 inches) deep. Prick the base with a fork and pop in the freezer for 30 minutes. Knead the trimmings into a ball, wrap in cling film and chill.

Line the pastry case with a sheet of foil, pressing it gently into the curves of the tin and folding it down carefully over the outside. Fill with baking beans and bake on the baking sheet for 15 minutes.

Remove the foil and beans, then bake for a further 5–10 minutes or until the pastry is firm and pale golden brown around the edges. If necessary, use a little beaten egg to brush over any cracks and return to the oven for 2–3 minutes to seal. Reduce the oven temperature to 180°C/350°F/Gas Mark 4.

Place the cooking apples in a medium saucepan with the cloves or star anise, butter, mixed spice, cinnamon and caster sugar. Cook, stirring, over a high heat until the apples are soft. Remove the cloves or star anise and cinnamon then add the dessert apples. Cool.

Spoon the cold apple mixture into the prepared flan case. Make pastry leaves and berries from the pastry trimmings and arrange over the apple filling to cover. Brush the pastry lightly with beaten egg and sprinkle with demerara sugar.

Bake on the baking sheet for 35 minutes or until golden brown and crisp. Leave to cool for 10 minutes before removing from the tin. Serve warm, dusted with a little extra sugar.

Tip The pastry cases and apple mixture can be made the day before and assembled ready for baking when needed. To store the cooked apples, press a sheet of cling film down over the surface to prevent discolouration.

Variation Use 350 g (12 oz) of dessert apples and stir in about 125 g (4½ oz) of blackberries or blueberries.

The stickiest toffee tart

Serves 8–10
Preparation time:
  40 minutes +
  30 minutes chilling +
  cooling
Cooking time:
  60–70 minutes

1 large quantity **Rich
  shortcrust pastry** (see
  Tip, page 8) or 500 g pack
  chilled **shortcrust pastry**
vanilla ice cream and fresh
  orange segments, to serve

Filling
175 g (6 oz) **dates**, pitted
125 g (4½ oz) **dark soft
  brown sugar**
50 g (1¾ oz) **unsalted butter**,
  diced
1 teaspoon **vanilla extract**
1 teaspoon **instant coffee
  granules**
2 large **eggs**, beaten
150 g (5½ oz) **plain flour**
½ teaspoon **bicarbonate of
  soda**
½ teaspoon **baking powder**

Toffee sauce
125 g (4½ oz) **light soft
  brown sugar**
75 g (2¾ oz) **butter**
300 ml (10 fl oz) **double cream**

Put a baking sheet in the oven and preheat to 200°C/400°F/Gas Mark 6.

Roll out the pastry on a lightly floured surface to about 3 mm (⅛ inch) thick, then use it to line a 23 cm (9 inch) loose-based, fluted flan tin, about 4.5–5 cm (1¾–2 inches) deep. Prick the base with a fork and pop it in the freezer for 30 minutes.

Line the pastry case with a sheet of foil, pressing it gently into the curves of the tin and folding it down carefully over the outside. Fill with baking beans and bake on the baking sheet for 15 minutes.

Remove the foil and beans, then bake for a further 5–10 minutes or until the pastry is firm and pale golden brown around the edges. If necessary, use a little beaten egg to brush over any cracks and return to the oven for 2–3 minutes to seal. Reduce the oven temperature to 190°C/375°F/Gas Mark 5.

For the filling, roughly chop the dates (see Tips) and put in a pan with the sugar and 175 ml (6 fl oz) of water. Simmer gently for about 10 minutes until the sugar has dissolved and the dates are very soft. Leave to cool, then blend in a food processor until smooth.

Add the butter, vanilla extract, coffee and eggs and whizz again until well blended. Scrape into a large mixing bowl.

Sift together the flour, bicarbonate of soda and baking powder, then gradually fold into the date mixture. Spoon into the pastry case and bake for 40–45 minutes, covering lightly with foil towards the end of the cooking time. A skewer inserted into the centre should come out clean.

Meanwhile, put the toffee sauce ingredients into a small saucepan and heat gently, stirring, until the sugar has dissolved. Simmer very gently for 2–3 minutes and keep warm.

Pierce the top of the tart all over with a fine skewer or cocktail stick and drizzle over a little of the warm sauce. Serve the tart warm, cut into slim wedges with vanilla ice cream, fresh orange segments and a jug of toffee sauce to hand round.

Tips Medjool dates are the best to use; they are in most supermarkets and good greengrocers now. It's worth seeking them out for their fudgy, toffee flavour. Instead of chopping them on a board, snip them with floured scissors straight into the saucepan.

The cooked tart will freeze well. Thaw for 1–2 hours then wrap loosely in foil and warm through in a moderate oven (180°C/350°F/Gas Mark 4). Drizzle with sauce as above.

Apple cider tray bake

Serves 12
Preparation time:
  35 minutes +
  10 minutes soaking +
  30 minutes chilling
Cooking time:
  70–80 minutes

1 large quantity **Rich
  shortcrust pastry** (see
  Tip, page 8) or 500 g pack
  chilled **shortcrust pastry**
125 g (4½ oz) blanched,
  toasted **hazelnuts**
250 g (9 oz) soft **unsalted
  butter**, plus extra for
  greasing
1 tablespoon **rolled oats**
75 g (2¾ oz) **light soft brown
  sugar**
200 g (7 oz) **plain flour**
50 ml (2 fl oz) **medium cider**
  or **apple juice**
350 g (12 oz) **cooking
  apples**, peeled, cored and
  cut into bite-size chunks
125 g (4½ oz) fresh **mango**,
  diced
200 g (7 oz) **caster sugar**
3 large **eggs**, beaten
2 teaspoons **baking powder**
5 tablespoons **soured cream**

Put a baking sheet in the oven and preheat
to 200°C/400°F/Gas Mark 6.

Roll out the pastry on a lightly floured surface
to about 3 mm (⅛ inch) thick, then use it to line
a 25 x 20 cm (10 x 8 inch) cake tin about 5 cm
(2 inches) deep. Prick the base and sides with
a fork and pop in the freezer for
30 minutes.

Line the pastry case with a sheet of foil,
pressing it gently into the corners of the tin
and folding it down carefully over the outside.
Cover the base with baking beans and bake
on the baking sheet for 15 minutes.

Remove the foil and beans, then bake for
a further 5–10 minutes or until the pastry is
firm and pale golden brown around the edges.
If necessary, use a little beaten egg to brush
over any cracks and return to the oven for
2–3 minutes to seal. Reduce the oven
temperature to 180C°/375°F/Gas Mark 4.

Put the nuts in a food processor and whizz for
2–3 seconds only, to chop roughly. Remove
25 g (1 oz) for the crumble topping then finely
grind the remainder for the cake mixture.

For the crumble, melt 25 g (1 oz) of the butter, add
the roughly chopped nuts, oats and brown sugar.
Stir in 50 g (1¾ oz) of the flour and set aside.

Stir the cider or apple juice into the apples
and mango and leave to soak for 10 minutes.

For the cake mixture, cream together the
remaining butter with the caster sugar until
light and fluffy. Gradually add the eggs, mixing
well after each addition. Mix together the
remaining flour with the baking powder and
reserved hazelnuts. Fold into the cake mixture,
along with the soured cream, until smooth.

Spread the cake mixture evenly into the
pastry case and bake for 30 minutes, then
drain the fruit and scatter over the cake
mixture. Sprinkle the crumble mix evenly over
the top and bake for a further 20–25 minutes
until golden brown and a skewer inserted into
the centre comes out clean. Cut into squares
to serve.

Tip Serve warm with custard or cold,
dusted with icing sugar.

Variations If you would rather, use
2 large cooking apples (about 450 g/1 lb),
instead of the mix of apples and mango.

Crumble 50 g (1¾ oz) of Lancashire cheese
into the pastry case with the apples.

Windfall pies

Gather up fallen apples and pears with some ripe blackberries and turn them into delicious little pies to keep on hand in the freezer.

Serves 6
Preparation time:
  50 minutes +
  30 minutes chilling +
  cooling
Cooking time:
  35–40 minutes

1 quantity **Soured cream cinnamon flaky pastry** (see Variation, page 12)

Filling
75 g (2¾ oz) **caster sugar**, plus extra to glaze
a pinch of **grated nutmeg**
½ teaspoon **ground cinnamon**
about 1.4 kg (3 lb) mixed **cooking apples** and **pears**, peeled, cored and cut into thick chunks
25 g (1 oz) **unsalted butter**
75 g (2¾ oz) ripe, clean **blackberries**
1 **egg yolk**, beaten with 2 teaspoons **water**
2 tablespoons **demerara sugar**, to glaze

Mix the sugar, nutmeg and cinnamon together in a large bowl. Add the apples and pears and stir to coat.

Melt half the butter in a wide, non-stick frying pan and add the fruit chunks. Fry over a high heat for about 5 minutes until beginning to soften a little but still retaining some bite. Transfer to a large bowl to cool completely. Put a baking sheet in the oven and preheat to 190°C/375°F/Gas Mark 5.

Cut about one-third off the pastry and set aside. Roll out the larger piece of pastry on a lightly floured surface to just under 3 mm (⅛ inch). Cut out six 15 cm (6 inch) rounds, re-rolling and using the trimmings. Use to line the bases and sides of a six-hole deep muffin tray. Prick the bases and freeze for 30 minutes.

Line the muffin cases with sheets of foil, pressing it into the edges and up and over the top. Put on the baking sheet and bake for 15 minutes until set and the top edges are golden. Leave to cool.

Ease the cooked cases out of the muffin tins. Put a 15 cm (6 inch) square of greaseproof paper over the muffin holes and gently ease the pastry case back in, pushing the paper down as you do so. Roll out the reserved pastry and stamp out six 9 cm (3½ inch) rounds.

Stir the blackberries into the cooled fruit and spoon into the pastry cases. Brush the pastry rim with the beaten egg and lay the pastry rounds on top to cover the pies. Trim and press the pastry edges firmly together to seal, then crimp with a fork. Brush the top with the egg, sprinkle with extra sugar and cut a small cross in the centre to allow the steam to escape during cooking.

Bake for 20–25 minutes until the crust is golden brown and crisp. Allow to stand for 15–20 minutes before serving.

Tips Pre-cooking the fruit means it has an intense caramel flavour and will not shrink during baking, creating pockets of air.

It's always worth blind baking the base pastry as it ensures the whole pie stays crisp.

The extra layer of greaseproof paper helps to lift the finished pies from the tins.

Boozy nut & maple tart

A must for nut lovers! Serve while it's still barely warm with crème fraîche to melt on top and extra maple syrup.

Serves 6–8
Preparation time:
 20 minutes +
 30 minutes chilling +
 1 hour cooling
Cooking time:
 65–70 minutes

200 g (7 oz) **nuts**, e.g.
 macadamia, hazelnut,
 walnut or pecans
1 quantity **Rich shortcrust
 pastry** (see page 8)
75 g (2¾ oz) **unsalted butter**,
 softened
75 g (2¾ oz) **dark soft brown
 sugar**
3 large **eggs**, beaten
1 teaspoon **cornflour**
50 ml (2 fl oz) **maple syrup**
225 ml (8 fl oz) **golden syrup**
grated zest of 1 **lemon**
4 tablespoons **whisky**,
 brandy or **lemon juice**
1 teaspoon **vanilla essence**

Put the nuts on a baking sheet and toast under a hot grill until golden brown. Leave to cool and roughly chop in half.

Put a baking sheet in the oven and preheat to 200°C/400°F/Gas Mark 6. Roll the pastry out on a lightly floured surface to about 3 mm (⅛ inch) thick and line a 23 cm (9 inch) loose-bottomed tart tin, 2.5 cm (1 inch) deep. Prick the base well with a fork then freeze for 30 minutes.

Line the pastry case with foil, pressing it gently into the corners of the tin and folding it down carefully over the outside. Cover the base with baking beans and cook for 15 minutes. Remove the foil and beans and cook for another 5–10 minutes until golden. If necessary, use a little beaten egg to brush over any cracks and return to the oven for 2–3 minutes to seal. Reduce the oven temperature to 180°C/375°F/Gas Mark 4.

To make the filling, beat the butter with the sugar until pale and creamy then slowly add the beaten eggs and cornflour (this is best done by hand to avoid getting too much air in the mixture). Stir in all the remaining ingredients. The mix will look curdled but don't panic. Stir in the toasted nuts and pour into the cooked pastry case.

Bake the tart for 45 minutes or until the filling is just set. Leave to cool for 1 hour before serving.

Tip The baked tart will freeze well. To use, thaw overnight at room temperature. Put it on a baking sheet, cover loosely with foil and reheat at 200°C/400°F/Gas Mark 6 for 20 minutes.

Sugar-roasted scrunch pie

A classic, American-style fruit pie with a crumbly crust folded round the fruit like a pasty. It takes no skill at all. Use a 375 g pack of ready-made chilled shortcrust pastry if you wish.

Serves 6–8
Preparation time:
 30 minutes +
 20 minutes cooling
Cooking time:
 40 minutes

50 g (1¾ oz) **Madeira cake**
1 quantity **Easiest pie pastry**
 (see page 10)
2–3 green **cardamom pods**
750 g (1 lb 10 oz) mixed
 yellow and **red plums**,
 or a mix of **red plums**
 and **apricots**, stoned and
 quartered
50 g (1¾ oz) **demerara** or
 caster sugar
1 small **egg**, beaten
icing sugar, for dusting
chilled **single cream** or
 vanilla ice cream, to
 serve

Put a baking sheet in the oven and preheat to 220°C/425°F/Gas Mark 7. Coarsely grate the cake into crumbs or whizz in a food processor.

Roll the pastry out on a lightly floured surface into a thin round about 30 cm (12 inches) in diameter. Put it on a second floured, flat baking sheet.

Split open the cardamom pods and crush or chop the seeds. Add to the fruit with 1 tablespoon of the sugar and stir well to coat.

Pile the cake crumbs into the centre of the pastry and spoon the fruit on top. Sprinkle with half the remaining sugar. Fold in the pastry edges and pinch to pleat together around the fruit. Brush the pastry with beaten egg and sprinkle with the remaining sugar.

Put the pie (and the cold baking sheet) on the hot baking sheet and bake for 10 minutes. Reduce the oven temperature to 170°C/325°F/Gas Mark 3 and continue to cook until the pastry is golden brown and a little charred at the edges, and the fruit is just tender, about 30 minutes. If the pastry begins to spread out of shape, simply push it back together with a palette knife.

Leave the pie to cool for 10 minutes, then carefully loosen the edge of the pastry from the baking sheet. Cool for a further 10 minutes before sliding the pie on to a serving plate or board. Serve warm, dusted with icing sugar and cut into wedges with single cream or ice cream.

Variation The point is to make the magical combination of pastry and fruit as simple as possible. Any fruit is suitable, try apricots, rhubarb, blackberries and pears, or a mix of summer berries with vanilla sugar or pears with ground cinnamon.

Lemon banana pies

Individual tartlet cases are useful for instant puddings. Make up a batch and keep in the freezer. Use a 375 g pack of ready-made chilled dessert pastry if you wish.

Makes 6
Preparation time:
  30 minutes +
  30 minutes chilling
Cooking time:
  40–45 minutes

1 quantity **Sweet flan pastry** (see page 9)

Filling
25 g (1 oz) toasted **walnuts**
100 g (3½ oz) **icing sugar**
40 g (1½ oz) **plain flour**
2 **egg whites**
½ teaspoon **vanilla extract**
100 g (3½ oz) **unsalted butter**, melted
1 small **banana** (about 100 g/3½ oz)
2 teaspoons **lemon juice**

Put a baking sheet in the oven and preheat to 200°C/400°F/Gas Mark 6. Roll out the pastry on a lightly floured surface to about 3 mm (⅛ inch) thick, then use it to line six 9 cm (3½ inch) round, 2 cm (¾ inch) deep, loose-based individual tartlet tins. Prick the bases with a fork and pop in the freezer for 30 minutes.

Line each pastry case with a small sheet of foil, pressing it gently into the curves of the tin and folding it down carefully over the outside. Fill the cases with baking beans and bake on the baking sheet for 10 minutes.

Remove the foil and beans, then bake for a further 10–15 minutes or until the pastry is firm and golden brown. If necessary, use a little beaten egg to brush over any cracks and return to the oven for 2–3 minutes to seal. Reduce the oven temperature to 170°C/325°F/Gas Mark 3.

Put the walnuts in a food processor with all but 1 tablespoon of the icing sugar and whizz to a fine powder. Add the flour and whizz for a few seconds more to combine. Add the egg whites and whizz again until just mixed. Then add the vanilla extract and melted butter and whizz again for a few seconds until just mixed together. Do this quickly in small bursts to avoid overworking the mixture.

Mash the banana with the lemon juice and remaining icing sugar and divide between the prepared tartlet cases. Spoon the walnut mixture on top and bake on the baking sheet for about 20 minutes, until the top is just firm to the touch. Serve warm.

Easy peasy pie

This pie is simplicity itself; it needs no tins, uses any fresh seasonal fruit and can be made ahead ready to pop in the oven. Perfect for a big family Sunday lunch.

Serves 8–10
Preparation time:
  25 minutes
Cooking time:
  30–35 minutes

1 quantity **Soured cream cinnamon flaky pastry** (see Variation, page 12)

Filling
125 g (4½ oz) **white almond paste**
450 g (1 lb) fresh **plums**, **apricots**, small **nectarines** or **peaches**, stoned and halved
icing sugar and chilled **crème fraîche**, to serve

Put a baking sheet in the oven and preheat to 180°C/350°F/Gas Mark 4. Cut one-third off the pastry block and return the remainder to the fridge. Roll the pastry out thinly on a lightly floured, non-stick baking sheet to make a rough circle about 20 cm (8 inches) in diameter.

Coarsely grate the almond paste over the pastry, leaving a clear edge about 1.25 cm (¼ inch) wide. Arrange the fruit over the almond paste, cut side down.

Roll out the reserved pastry and drape over the top, allowing it to sink down into the gaps between the fruit pieces. Press the two layers of pastry together.

Bake on the baking sheet for about 30–35 minutes. Serve dusted with icing sugar with chilled crème fraîche.

Tip The pastry is very forgiving; any cracks can be simply patched up.

Variation Any pastry can be used for this pie. Use two ready-made sheets of shortcrust pastry and the pie can be made in minutes!

Double crust apple pie

English Bramley apples have to be the first choice for a traditional pie, but try other combinations such as pears and blackberries or rhubarb and ginger.

Serves 6
Preparation time:
 50 minutes +
 30 minutes chilling +
 cooling
Cooking time:
 30–40 minutes

1 quantity **Rich shortcrust pastry** (see page 8)
finely grated zest and juice of 1 **lemon** or **orange**
450 g (1 lb) **fruit**, e.g. Bramley apples
225 g (8 oz) **Cox's apples** or **pears**
50 g (1¾ oz) **soft light brown sugar**
1 tablespoon **plain flour**
¼ teaspoon **mixed spice**
1 **clove**
50 g (1¾ oz) **sultanas**
25 g (1 oz) **butter**
a little **milk**, for brushing
caster sugar, for sprinkling

Put a baking sheet in the oven and preheat to 190°C/375°F/Gas Mark 5. Roll out two-thirds of the pastry on a lightly floured surface to about 3 mm (⅛ inch) thick and use to line a 20 cm (8 inch) deep pie dish, leaving any excess overhanging the sides. Chill in the freezer for 30 minutes.

Add the lemon or orange juice to a bowl of cold water. Peel, core and thickly slice the fruit into the water; this will stop the apples turning brown.

Mix together the citrus zest, sugar, flour and spices, and sprinkle a little on to the pastry-lined dish.

Drain the apples thoroughly and pat dry with kitchen towel. Cover the pastry base with half the apples, sprinkle with half the sultanas and half the remaining sugar mixture. Repeat with the remaining ingredients and dot with the butter.

Brush the pastry edge with a little milk or water. Roll out the remaining pastry and cut into rough rectangular shapes. Lay over the apple mixture, slightly overlapping. Leave a small hole in the centre to allow steam to escape. Seal the edges well and trim any excess with a sharp knife. Brush with milk and sprinkle with caster sugar.

Place on the baking sheet and bake for 30–40 minutes, until golden brown. Cool for 10–15 minutes before serving. Serve hot or cold.

Variations
Omit the clove and add the crushed seeds of 1 whole cardamom pod.

Throw in a handful of blackberries or blueberries with the fruit.

If you prefer, cover the fruit with one large sheet of pastry in the traditional way.

Rhubarb crumbly tarts

The perfect recipe to make the most of new season rhubarb. If you don't have a muffin tray, lay the pastry over inverted, buttered ceramic ramekins.

Serves 6
Preparation time:
45 minutes +
30 minutes chilling +
overnight soaking
Cooking time:
25–35 minutes

450 g (1 lb) **rhubarb**
125 g (4½ oz) **caster sugar**
150 g (5½ oz) **unsalted butter**
125 g (4½ oz) chilled **filo pastry**
150 g (5½ oz) **plain flour**
25 g (1 oz) **flaked almonds**
vanilla custard, to serve
icing sugar, for dusting

Peel any coarse strings off the rhubarb and cut the flesh into bite-size pieces. Mix with 50 g (1¾ oz) of the caster sugar, cover and leave in a cool place overnight.

Put a baking sheet in the oven and preheat to 190°C/375°F/Gas Mark 5. Melt 25 g (1 oz) of the butter.

Cut the filo pastry into 18 x 15 cm (6 inch) squares. Brush a square with a little of the melted butter and press down firmly into one hole of a six-hole deep muffin tin. Lay two more pieces of buttered pastry on top and press down. Repeat with all the other muffin holes. Chill for 30 minutes.

Put the muffin tin on the hot baking sheet and bake the cases for 5 minutes or until the pastry is golden and crisp. Cool for 5 minutes before easing out of the tins on to the baking sheet.

To make the crumble, rub the remaining butter into the flour until the mixture resembles fine breadcrumbs and then stir in the remaining sugar and the flaked almonds.

Drain the rhubarb, reserving any juices (see Tip). Spoon about 1 tablespoon of crumble mixture into each pastry. Spoon in the rhubarb and sprinkle over the remaining crumble mix.

Bake for 20–30 minutes or until the crumble is golden brown. Serve with vanilla custard and dusted with icing sugar.

Tip These are delicious served with a syrup sauce, made by simmering 3 tablespoons of golden syrup with the juice of 3 oranges, any reserved rhubarb juice and 200 ml (7 fl oz) of water for 10 minutes. Off the heat, stir in 2–3 tablespoons of double cream.

Variation Any fruit can be used in these little crumbles; try apple and raspberry, black cherry or fresh figs.

Spiced ginger loaf

Serves 10–12
Preparation time:
  **30 minutes + chilling
  + cooling**
Cooking time:
  70–75 minutes

1 large quantity **Sweet flan
  pastry** (see Tips, page
  9) or 1½ x 375 g packs
  chilled **dessert pastry**
300 g (10½ oz) **dark soft
  brown sugar**
2 large **eggs**
175 ml (6 fl oz) **vegetable oil**
200 g (7 oz) **wholemeal flour**
4 tablespoons finely
  chopped **stem ginger**
1 teaspoon **baking powder**
1 teaspoon **bicarbonate of
  soda**
225 g (8 oz) **carrots**
grated zest of 1 small
  orange
75 g (2¾ oz) dried **cherries**
50 g (1¾ oz) **desiccated
  coconut**

Topping
juice of ½ small **orange**
2 tablespoons **lemon juice**
150 ml (5 fl oz) **double cream**
225 g (8 oz) **mascarpone**
1 teaspoon **icing sugar**
2 teaspoons **maple syrup**

Put a baking sheet in the oven and preheat
to 200°C/400°F/Gas Mark 6.

Roll out the pastry on a lightly floured surface
to about 3 mm (⅛ inch) thick and use to line
the base and sides of a 30 x 20 cm (12 x
8 inch) loose-based fluted flan tin, 4.5–5 cm
(1¾–2 inches) deep. Prick the base and sides
and freeze for 30 minutes.

Line the pastry with a sheet of foil, pressing
it well into the corner and folding up and over
the top edge. Fill the case with baking beans,
place on the baking sheet and bake for
25–30 minutes. Remove the foil and beans.
Reduce the oven temperature to 170°C/325°F/
Gas Mark 3.

Put 175 g (6 oz) of the dark brown sugar in a
bowl with the eggs and oil. Beat together for
3–4 minutes until thoroughly mixed. Stir in the
flour, ginger, baking powder and bicarbonate
of soda. Grate the carrots and stir in with the
orange zest, cherries and coconut.

Spoon the mixture into the pastry case and
bake for about 45 minutes or until the cake is
risen and golden and a skewer inserted into
the centre comes out clean.

Whisk the remaining sugar and orange and
lemon juice together in a bowl. As soon as you
remove the tart from the oven, skewer it all
over, then spoon the sugary orange liquid over
the warm tart until it's completely absorbed.
Leave to cool in the tin before turning out.

Beat together the cream, mascarpone, icing
sugar and 1 teaspoon of the maple syrup.
Cover and chill. Spread the top of the tart
with the mascarpone frosting, drizzle with
the remaining maple syrup and slice to serve.

Tip The tart can be frozen without the icing.
Thaw overnight and ice as above.

Variation Dried cranberries
or blueberries can be used instead of
the cherries.

Honey puff tarts

These simple little tarts are made in minutes and are the perfect way for children to help out in the kitchen. Serve with ice cream.

Makes 4
Preparation time:
   15 minutes
Cooking time:
   20 minutes

200 g (7 oz) chilled **puff pastry**
1 small **egg**, beaten
2 large ripe **plums**, **peaches** or **nectarines**, halved and stoned
1 tablespoon **clear honey**
2 teaspoons **butter**

Put a baking sheet in the oven and preheat to 220°C/425°F/Gas Mark 7. Thinly roll out the pastry on a lightly floured surface. Stamp out four 10 cm (4 inch) diameter rounds, or cut out using a cup or mug as a guide.

Arrange the rounds on a second baking sheet. Brush each round with beaten egg and place a fruit half on top, cut side down. Using half the honey, drizzle a little over each piece of fruit, then dot with butter.

Put the second baking sheet on the heated baking sheet and bake for 20 minutes or until the fruit is soft and the pastry is puffed and golden.

Drizzle the remaining honey over each piece of fruit to glaze and serve warm.

Variations
Try peeled, halved and cored apples or pears, halved and stoned apricots or thick rounds of banana.

Slip a flat round of white marzipan under each fruit half before baking.

Raspberry & nectarine tart

Make this at the height of summer when the fruit is at its best. It's very simple but full of flavour.

Serves 6–8
Preparation time:
  30 minutes +
  30 minutes chilling
Cooking time:
  50–55 minutes

1 quantity **Rich orange shortcrust pastry** (see Variation, page 8)

Filling
350 g (12 oz) **raspberries** or **blueberries**
75 g (2¾ oz) **caster sugar**
2 tablespoons **orange juice**, **ginger wine** or **crème de cassis**
2 ripe **nectarines** or **peaches**, halved, stoned and thinly sliced
50 g (1¾ oz) **plain flour**
1 tablespoon **cornflour**
25 g (1 oz) **butter**
50 g (1¾ oz) chopped **walnuts**
icing sugar, for dusting
single cream, to serve

Put a baking sheet in the oven and preheat to 200°C/400°F/Gas Mark 6. Roll out the pastry on a lightly floured surface to about 3 mm (⅛ inch) thick, then use it to line a 23 cm (9 inch) loose-based, fluted flan tin, about 2.5 cm (1 inch) deep. Prick the base with a fork and pop in the freezer for 30 minutes.

Line the pastry case with a sheet of foil, pressing it gently into the curves of the tin and folding it down carefully over the outside. Fill with baking beans and bake on the baking sheet for 15 minutes.

Remove the foil and beans, then bake for a further 5–10 minutes or until the pastry is firm and pale golden brown around the edges. If necessary, use a little beaten egg to brush over any cracks and return to the oven for 2–3 minutes to seal.

Put the raspberries in a bowl with 50 g (1¾ oz) of the caster sugar and the orange juice, ginger wine or crème de cassis. Gently stir in the nectarines or peaches, trying to avoid breaking up the fruit. Set aside.

Put the flour, cornflour and butter in a food processor and whizz until the mixture resembles fine breadcrumbs. Stir in the remaining sugar and walnuts.

Fill the pastry case with the raspberry and nectarine mixture. Spoon the flour mixture on top, leaving the fruit peeping through in places.

Bake on the baking sheet for 30 minutes or until the topping is golden brown. Dust with icing sugar and serve warm with single cream.

Tip The pastry case, fruit and topping can be made the day before needed and assembled and baked on the day.

Variation Make the same tart in the autumn with blackberries and ripe pears.

Blueberry bay tart

Make the most of seasonal fruit with this unusual and delicious tart. Bay leaves add a subtle fragrance to the blueberries.

Serves 8
Preparation time:
  35 minutes +
  30 minutes chilling +
  cooling
Cooking time:
  20–25 minutes

1 quantity **Sweet flan pastry**
  (see page 9)
450 g (1 lb) **blueberries**
100 g (3½ oz) **caster sugar**
finely grated zest and juice
  of 1 **lemon**
2 **bay leaves**
25 g (1 oz) **cornflour**
450 ml (16 fl oz) **milk**
3 **egg yolks**
a few drops **vanilla extract**
8 tablespoons **redcurrant
  jelly**

Put a baking sheet in the oven and preheat to 200°C/400°F/Gas Mark 6. Roll out the pastry on a lightly floured surface to about 3 mm (⅛ inch) thick, then use it to line a 23 cm (9 inch) loose-based, fluted flan tin, about 2.5 cm (1 inch) deep. Prick the base with a fork and pop in the freezer for 30 minutes.

Line the pastry case with a sheet of foil, pressing it gently into the curves of the tin and folding it down carefully over the outside. Fill with baking beans and bake on the baking sheet for 15 minutes.

Remove the foil and beans, then bake for a further 5–10 minutes or until the pastry is firm and pale golden brown around the edges. If necessary, use a little beaten egg to brush over any cracks and return to the oven for 2–3 minutes to seal.

Place the blueberries in a medium lidded saucepan. Add 50 g (1¾ oz) of the caster sugar, the lemon zest, bay leaf and 150 ml (5 fl oz) of cold water. Bring slowly to the boil and simmer, uncovered, for 1–2 minutes. Leave to cool.

In a medium bowl, mix the cornflour to a smooth paste with a little of the milk and add the egg yolks. Heat the remaining milk gently with the remaining sugar and vanilla extract, stirring for 1–2 minutes or until the sugar has dissolved. Bring to the boil and pour over the egg mixture. Stir well, then strain into the rinsed-out saucepan. Return to the boil, then simmer, stirring, for 2–3 minutes or until thickened. Pour into a bowl, cover with damp greaseproof paper and leave to cool.

Spoon the cold custard mixture evenly into the prepared flan case. Drain the blueberries and spoon them over the custard.

In a small saucepan, melt the redcurrant jelly with 2 tablespoons of lemon juice. Bring to the boil, then brush the hot glaze over the blueberries as evenly as possible to cover the fruit completely. Serve within 1 hour.

Cornish slice

A traditional fruit pastry from the West Country; it is delicious served cold with coffee or warm with custard.

Serves 10–12
Preparation time:
  20 minutes +
  20 minutes chilling +
  cooling
Cooking time:
  50 minutes

75 g (2¾ oz) mixed **dried fruit**

75 g (2¾ oz) **dried figs**, roughly chopped

2 teaspoons **mixed spice**

150 ml (5 fl oz) boiling **water**

450 g (1 lb) chilled **puff pastry**

150 g (5½ oz) **cake crumbs**, e.g. Madeira sponge or trifle sponges

a pinch of **allspice** (optional)

1 **egg**, beaten

2 tablespoons **caster sugar**

Mix together the dried fruit, figs and spice. Pour over the boiling water. Set aside overnight.

Preheat the oven to 200°C/400°F/Gas Mark 6. Roll out half the pastry on a lightly floured surface to a thin 25 cm (10 inch) square. Put on a baking sheet, prick with a fork and chill for about 20 minutes.

Bake the pastry base for 10 minutes, remove from the oven and prick again to expel all the air. Return to the oven for a further 10 minutes until golden brown, then leave to cool.

Stir the cake crumbs into the dried fruit mixture to make a thick paste and spread it evenly over the pastry base to within 1.25 cm (½ inch) of the edge. Brush the edge lightly with beaten egg.

Roll out the remaining pastry to a square slightly larger than the first and lay over the fruit filling. Press the edges together to seal and prick several holes in the top of the pastry with a fork. Brush with beaten egg and sprinkle with the caster sugar.

Bake for about 30 minutes or until golden brown. Serve warm or cold, cut into squares.

Tip Baking the pastry base first ensures a good crisp bottom to the finished slice.

Summer tartlets

Gorgeous nutty tartlet cases filled with peaches and cream – perfect for pudding on a summer's day and so quick to assemble.

Serves 6
Preparation time:
  20 minutes +
  30 minutes chilling +
  cooling
Cooking time:
  20–25 minutes

1 quantity **Sweet nut pastry** (see page 11)
125 ml (4 fl oz) good quality chilled **custard**
200 g tub **mascarpone**
6 tablespoons **peach conserve**
450 g (1 lb) mixed **summer berries**, plus 2–3 fresh **figs**, cut into wedges
icing sugar, for dusting (optional)

Put a baking sheet in the oven and preheat to 200°C/400°F/Gas Mark 6. Roll out the pastry on a lightly floured surface to about 3 mm (⅛ inch) thick, then use it to line six 9 cm (3½ inch), 2 cm (¾ inch) deep, loose-based individual tartlet tins. Prick the bases with a fork and pop in the freezer for 30 minutes.

Line each pastry case with a small sheet of foil, pressing it gently into the curves of the tin and folding it down carefully over the outside. Fill the cases with baking beans and bake on the baking sheet for 10 minutes.

Remove the foil and beans, then bake for a further 10–15 minutes or until the pastry is firm and golden brown. If necessary, use a little beaten egg to brush over any cracks and return to the oven for 2–3 minutes to seal. Leave to cool.

Gradually beat the custard into the mascarpone until soft and creamy and the texture of whipped cream.

Spread the base of each cold tartlet case with peach conserve. Spoon the mascarpone mixture on top and finish with a mix of berries and a wedge of fig. Dust with icing sugar, if using, and serve.

Variation
Top the peach conserve with scoops of vanilla ice cream and a tumble of summer berries.

Sweet brunch cups

There's something very special about having friends to brunch on a Sunday morning. These breakfast cups can be assembled ready to bake the day before.

Serves 6
Preparation time:
  30 minutes + cooling
Cooking time:
  20–25 minutes

450 g (1 lb) **rhubarb**, trimmed and cut into 2.5 cm (1 inch) lengths
50 g (1¾ oz) **caster sugar**
juice of 1 **lemon**
2 tablespoons **honey**
2.5 cm (1 inch) **fresh root ginger**, peeled and finely grated
3 ripe **pears**, peeled, cored and thickly sliced
225 g (8 oz) chilled **puff pastry**
a little beaten **egg**
demerara sugar, for sprinkling
Greek yogurt, to serve

Mix together the rhubarb, sugar, lemon juice, honey and ginger in a small saucepan. Cook over a gentle heat until the rhubarb begins to soften. Stir in the pears and leave to cool.

Roll out the puff pastry on a lightly floured surface to about 3 mm (⅛ inch) thick. Cut six 2.5 cm (1 inch) wide strips and fit them over the rims of six large heatproof breakfast cups or individual pie dishes. Cut out six rounds using the cup saucers as a template.

Preheat the oven to 200°C/400°F/Gas Mark 6. Spoon the cold fruit mixture into the cups or dishes.

Brush the top edge of the cups with beaten egg and top with the pastry rounds. Press down on to the edge of the cup to seal. Brush with more beaten egg and sprinkle heavily with demerara sugar. Make two holes in the top of each lid to allow steam to escape.

Put the cups in a large roasting tin and fill with enough hot water to come half way up the sides of the cups. Bake for 20–25 minutes or until puffed and golden brown.

Serve the hot cups on saucers with a bowl of Greek yogurt to spoon in when the pies are broken into.

Cherry cinnamon pie

To turn a simple cherry pie into something special, add some chopped quince jelly (membrillo) before baking.

Serves 6–8
Preparation time:
  25 minutes +
  20 minutes
  marinating
Cooking time:
  45 minutes

1 tablespoon **cornflour**
25 g (1 oz) **caster sugar**
50 g (1¾ oz) **quince jelly**, roughly chopped (optional)
a pinch of **ground cinnamon** or **mixed spice**
900 g (2 lb) fresh **cherries**, stoned
1 quantity **Sweet nut pastry** (see page 11)
25 g (1 oz) fresh **white breadcrumbs**
1 tablespoon **milk**, for brushing
2 tablespoons **granulated sugar**

Mix the cornflour, caster sugar, quince jelly (if using) and cinnamon or mixed spice together, then gently toss with the cherries in a bowl. Set aside for 20 minutes. Put a baking sheet in the oven and preheat to 190°C/375°F/Gas Mark 5.

Roll the pastry out on a lightly floured surface to about 3 mm (⅛ inch) thick and use to line a 1.7 litre (3 pint), 5 cm (2 inch) deep ovenproof dish. There should be about 2.5 cm (1 inch) of pastry over-hanging the sides. Sprinkle the pastry with the breadcrumbs then top with the cherry mixture. Loosely fold the pastry over the cherries. It should NOT meet in the middle. Brush with milk and sprinkle with the granulated sugar.

Bake on the baking sheet for about 45 minutes until the fruit is soft and the pastry is golden brown. Serve warm.

Mississippi mud pie

Serves 12
Preparation time:
 **70 minutes + at least
 3½ hours chilling +
 cooling**
Cooking time:
 20–25 minutes

1 quantity **Chocolate
 hazelnut crust** (see page
 10), chilled, or 1½ x
 375 g packs chilled
 dessert pastry
450 ml (16 fl oz) **double
 cream**
225 g (8 oz) **caster sugar**
2 tablespoons **cornflour**
4 large **eggs**, 2 lightly
 beaten, 2 separated
50 g (1¾ oz) chilled **unsalted
 butter**, diced
a few drops of **vanilla
 extract**
1 tablespoon **coffee cream
 liqueur**
1 teaspoon **coffee essence**
 or 1 teaspoon **instant
 coffee granules** mixed
 with 1 teaspoon boiling
 water
125 g (4½ oz) **plain
 chocolate**, broken into
 pieces
chocolate shards (see Tip),
 to decorate

Put a baking sheet in the oven and preheat to 180°C/350°F/Gas Mark 4. Roll out the pastry on a lightly floured surface to about 3 mm (⅛ inch) thick, then use it to line a 23 cm (9 inch) loose-based, fluted flan tin, about 4.5–5 cm (1¾–2 inches) deep. Prick the base with a fork and pop in the freezer for 30 minutes.

Line the pastry case with a sheet of foil, pressing it gently into the curves of the tin and folding it down carefully over the outside. Fill with baking beans and bake on the baking sheet for 15 minutes. Remove the foil and beans, then bake for a further 5–10 minutes or until the pastry is firm, pale golden brown and cooked through.

Place 300 ml (10 fl oz) of the cream and the sugar in a heavy-based, non-stick saucepan and, stirring occasionally, heat very gently until the sugar has completely dissolved – at least 5 minutes. Remove from the heat.

Mix the cornflour to a smooth paste with 2 tablespoons of cold water. Stir the cornflour and beaten eggs into the cream and sugar and beat until combined and smooth. Return to the heat and slowly bring to the boil, stirring constantly, until very thick and smooth. This will take about 10 minutes.

Beat the butter into the fudge mixture a little at a time with the vanilla extract, coffee cream liqueur and coffee essence until well combined and the mixture is very smooth and creamy. Pour over the pastry base, allow to cool, then freeze for at least 1 hour to set.

Place the chocolate in a small bowl over a saucepan of gently simmering water. Heat slowly until melted, smooth and shiny. Whisk the egg yolks and remaining cream together, add to the chocolate and whisk until smooth. Place over a low heat and stir constantly until the mixture thickly coats the back of a wooden spoon, about 10 minutes. Do not boil or the mixture will curdle. Remove from the heat, press a damp piece of greaseproof paper over the surface and leave to cool completely.

Lightly whisk the egg whites until they just form soft peaks. Stir about one-third into the chocolate mixture, then gently fold in the remainder. Pour the chocolate mixture evenly over the fudge filling, levelling the surface if necessary. Return to the freezer until solid – at least 2–3 hours or overnight. Decorate with chocolate shards and serve straight from the freezer, cutting with a hot knife.

Tip To make chocolate shards, brush a square of baking parchment lightly with melted milk chocolate. Roll the paper up into a scroll and freeze for 1 hour. Unroll and the chocolate will break into shards as it falls off the parchment. Store in the freezer.

Chocolate cappuccino tarts

A deliciously creamy mocha custard fills crisp pastry tartlets, making the perfect finale to a winter menu.

Serves 6
Preparation time:
  30 minutes + at least
  3½ hours chilling
Cooking time:
  25 minutes

1 quantity **Sweet nut pastry**
  (see page 11), made with
  hazelnuts
2 small **egg yolks**, plus
  1 **egg white**
25 g (1 oz) **caster sugar**
75 g (2¾ oz) **plain**
  chocolate, broken into
  pieces
100 ml (3½ fl oz) black
  coffee
300 ml (10 fl oz) **double**
  cream

To decorate
chocolate curls (see Tip)
cocoa powder, for dusting

Put a baking sheet in the oven and preheat to 200°C/400°F/Gas Mark 6. Roll out the pastry on a lightly floured surface to about 3 mm (⅛ inch) thick, then use it to line six 9 cm (3½ inch) round, 3 cm (1½ inch) deep, loose-based individual fluted tartlet tins. Prick the bases with a fork and pop in the freezer for 30 minutes.

Line each pastry case with a small sheet of foil, pressing it gently into the curves of the tin and folding it down carefully over the outside. Fill the cases with baking beans and bake on the baking sheet for 15 minutes.

Remove the foil and beans, then bake for a further 10 minutes or until the pastry is firm, golden brown and cooked through. If necessary, use a little beaten egg to brush over any cracks and return to the oven for 2–3 minutes to seal.

Beat the egg yolks with the caster sugar until well mixed. Place the chocolate, coffee and 125 ml (4 fl oz) of double cream in a medium saucepan, place over a low heat and cook, stirring, until the chocolate has melted.

Pour the chocolate cream over the egg yolk mixture, stirring all the time, then return to the saucepan. Cook, stirring, over a medium heat, until the mixture forms a custard that is thick enough to coat the back of a spoon. Do not boil.

Pour the mixture into the cooled tart cases and chill for at least 3 hours or overnight to allow the custard to set.

Remove the pastry cases from the flan tins. Whip the remaining cream until it just holds its shape. Whisk the egg white until it forms soft peaks and fold into the cream. Decorate the tarts with a dollop of frothy cream, chocolate curls and a dusting of cocoa powder.

Tip For easy chocolate curls, use plain chocolate (stored at room temperature) and, using a swivel vegetable peeler, pare off curls.

Variation For a lighter pudding, make the tartlet cases with filo pastry (see Panna cotta fig flans, page 102).

Spiced pear tart

Marinated pears baked in a rich chocolate filling. Serve this delicious tart at any special occasion. Use 1½ x 375 g packs of ready-made chilled dessert pastry if you wish.

Serves 8
Preparation time:
  60 minutes +
  30 minutes chilling +
  cooling
Cooking time:
  55–70 minutes

1 large quantity **Sweet flan pastry** (see Tip, page 9)

Poached pears
6 **Comice pears**, ripe but firm, peeled
juice of 1 **lemon**
juice of 1 **orange**
225 g (8 oz) **caster sugar**
1 **cinnamon stick**
600 ml (20 fl oz) **white wine**

Chocolate filling
175 g (6 oz) **milk chocolate**, broken into pieces
175 ml (6 fl oz) **double cream**
75 g (2¾ oz) **light soft brown sugar**
2 **eggs**, beaten
1 tablespoon **Grand Marnier** or **Cointreau**

Put a baking sheet in the oven and preheat to 200°C/400°F/Gas Mark 6. Roll out the pastry on a lightly floured surface to about 3 mm (⅛ inch) thick, then use it to line a 23 cm (9 inch) loose-based, fluted flan tin, about 4.5–5 cm (1¾–2 inches) deep. Prick the base with a fork and pop in the freezer for 30 minutes.

Line the pastry case with a sheet of foil, pressing it gently into the curves of the tin and folding it down carefully over the outside. Fill with baking beans and bake on the baking sheet for 15 minutes.

Remove the foil and beans, and bake for a further 5–10 minutes or until the pastry is firm and pale golden brown around the edges. If necessary, use a little beaten egg to brush over any cracks and return to the oven for 2–3 minutes to seal. Reduce the oven temperature to 170°C/325°F/Gas Mark 3.

Put the pears into a saucepan with all the other poaching ingredients and 600 ml (20 fl oz) of water. Bring to the boil then lower the heat and poach for about 20 minutes until cooked all the way through but not soft. Leave to marinate in the liquid until cold.

Melt the chocolate in a heatproof bowl over a pan of simmering water. Leave to cool for 10 minutes.

Put the cream, sugar, eggs and liqueur into a bowl and stir, using a wooden spoon, to mix thoroughly. Slowly stir in the melted chocolate.

Drain the pears, core and quarter. Arrange the fruit in the pastry case, thinner ends pointing inwards, then pour over the chocolate mixture.

Bake the tart for 35–45 minutes until just set.

Tips This is wonderful either warm or cold: cut it into slices, dust liberally with icing sugar and serve with crème fraîche.

Chill or freeze the pear poaching liquid to use in winter fruit salads.

Salted caramel tarts

A classic chocolate and orange combination with the added flavour of rich, salty caramel. Use a 375 g pack of ready-made chilled shortcrust pastry if you wish.

Serves 6
Preparation time:
40 minutes +
30 minutes chilling +
cooling
Cooking time:
30–35 minutes

1 quantity **Rich shortcrust pastry** (see page 8)

Salted caramel
50 g (1¾ oz) **caster sugar**
25 g (1 oz) blanched **almonds**
¼ teaspoon fine **sea salt**

Filling
75 g (2¾ oz) **plain** or **milk chocolate**
75 ml (3 fl oz) **double cream**
40 g (1½ oz) **light soft brown sugar**
1 large **egg**, beaten
2 teaspoons **Cointreau** or **Grand Marnier**

Put a baking sheet in the oven and preheat to 200°C/400°F/Gas Mark 6. Roll out the pastry on a lightly floured surface to about 3 mm (⅛ inch) thick, then use it to line six 9 cm (3½ inch) round, 3 cm (1¼ inch) deep, loose-based individual tartlet tins. Prick the bases with a fork and pop in the freezer for 30 minutes.

Line each pastry case with a small sheet of foil, pressing it gently into the curves of the tin and folding it down carefully over the outside. Fill the cases with baking beans and bake on the baking sheet for 10 minutes.

Remove the foil and beans, then bake for a further 5–10 minutes or until the pastry is firm and golden brown. If necessary, use a little beaten egg to brush over any cracks and return to the oven for 2–3 minutes to seal. Reduce the oven temperature to 170°C/325°F/Gas Mark 3.

To make the salted caramel, put the sugar in a saucepan and melt very slowly to a dark caramel colour. Stir in the almonds and salt and pour on to a non-stick baking sheet. Leave to cool and set for 20 minutes, then break into chunks and whizz to a rough powder in a food processor. Set aside.

Melt the chocolate in a heatproof bowl over a pan of gently simmering water. Leave to cool for 10 minutes.

Put the cream, sugar, egg and liqueur into a bowl and stir, with a wooden spoon, to mix thoroughly. Slowly stir in the melted chocolate then pour the mixture into the pastry cases. Bake for about 15 minutes until just set.

Serve the tarts warm with a dusting of the salted caramel.

Tips The caramel will keep in an airtight container for 2–3 days.

The baked tarts will freeze. To use, thaw overnight at room temperature. Warm in a low oven for 10 minutes before serving.

Chocolate cinnamon flan

An impressive pudding that takes a little time to do but can be made ahead and frozen. Use a 375 g pack of ready-made chilled shortcrust pastry if you wish.

Serves 6–8
Preparation time:
70 minutes +
90 minutes chilling +
cooling
Cooking time:
20–25 minutes

1 large quantity **Rich shortcrust pastry** (see Tip, page 8)
300 ml (10 fl oz) whole **milk**
4–5 drops **vanilla extract**
1 level tablespoon **powdered gelatine**
3 **eggs**, separated
125 g (4½ oz) **caster sugar**
50 g (1¾ oz) **plain chocolate**, roughly chopped
½ teaspoon **ground cinnamon**
chocolate leaves (see Tips), to decorate
cocoa powder, for dusting

Put a baking sheet in the oven and preheat to 200°C/400°F/Gas Mark 6.

Roll out the pastry on a lightly floured surface to about 3 mm (⅛ inch) thick, then use it to line a 23 cm (9 inch) loose-based, fluted flan tin, about 4.5–5 cm (1¾–2 inches) deep. Prick the base with a fork and pop in the freezer for 30 minutes.

Line the pastry case with a sheet of foil, pressing it gently into the curves of the tin and folding it down carefully over the outside. Fill with baking beans and bake on the baking sheet for 15 minutes.

Remove the foil and beans, then bake for a further 5–10 minutes or until the pastry is firm, pale golden brown round the edges and cooked through. If necessary, use a little beaten egg to brush over any cracks and return to the oven for 2–3 minutes to seal.

Put the milk and vanilla extract in a saucepan and bring to the boil.

Sprinkle the gelatine over 3 tablespoons of water in a small bowl and leave to soak for 2–3 minutes. Place the bowl over a pan of gently simmering water and leave until dissolved and clear, about 5 minutes.

Whisk together the egg yolks and 75 g (2¾ oz) of the caster sugar until very pale and thick. Pour the hot milk on to the egg mixture, whisking constantly. Return the mixture to the pan and heat gently, without boiling, until it thickens enough to coat the back of a wooden spoon. Off the heat, stir in the dissolved gelatine. Add the chocolate and stir until melted. Add the cinnamon and cool until just beginning to set.

Whisk the egg whites until they form stiff peaks, add the remaining caster sugar and whisk again until stiff. Fold the meringue into the custard and spoon into the pastry case. Freeze for about 1 hour to set quickly. Decorate with chocolate leaves and a dusing of cocoa powder and chill until ready to serve.

Tips Wrap the frozen flan and keep in the freezer. To use, thaw in the fridge for 3–4 hours.

To make chocolate leaves, lightly brush the underside of clean rose leaves with melted milk and white chocolate and chill to set. Carefully peel off the leaves. Keep frozen in a rigid container.

Double choc cheesecake

Deliciously rich as all chocolate puddings should be. This is an irresistible treat and perfect for special occasions.

Serves 8
Preparation time:
30 minutes + at least
3½ hours chilling +
cooling
Cooking time:
70–75 minutes

1 quantity **Sweet nut pastry** (see page 11), made with walnuts

Filling
125 g (4½ oz) **plain chocolate**, broken into pieces
125 g (4½ oz) **white chocolate**, broken into pieces
400 g (14 oz) **full fat soft cheese**
125 g (4½ oz) **caster sugar**
3 large **eggs**, beaten
finely grated zest of
   1 orange
150 ml (5 fl oz) **double cream**
icing sugar, for dusting
single cream or **custard**, to serve

Put a baking sheet in the oven and preheat to 200°C/400°F/Gas Mark 6. Roll out the pastry on a lightly floured surface to about 3 mm (⅛ inch) thick, then use it to line a 23 cm (9 inch) loose-based, fluted flan tin, about 4.5–5 cm (1¾–2 inches) deep. Prick the base with a fork and pop in the freezer for 30 minutes.

Line the pastry case with a sheet of foil, pressing it gently into the curves of the tin and folding it down carefully over the outside. Fill with baking beans and bake on the baking sheet for 15 minutes.

Remove the foil and beans, then bake for a further 5–10 minutes or until the pastry is firm and pale golden brown around the edges. If necessary, use a little beaten egg to brush over any cracks and return to the oven for 2–3 minutes to seal. Reduce the oven temperature to 180°C/350°F/Gas Mark 4.

Put the plain and white chocolate into two separate bowls and melt slowly over pans of simmering water or in the microwave. Cool until barely warm but still liquid.

Beat together the cheese and sugar in a large bowl until smooth, then gradually beat in the eggs, orange zest and cream. Divide the mixture between two bowls. Stir the melted plain chocolate into one and the melted white chocolate into the other.

Spoon the plain chocolate mixture into the cooked pastry case and smooth with a palette knife. Cover with the white chocolate mixture and smooth again.

Bake the tart for 50 minutes or until the filling is just set around the edges. Leave to cool in the tin then chill to set for about 3 hours or overnight.

Turn out the chilled tart, dust with icing sugar and serve with single cream or custard.

Variation Fold 1 teaspoon of liqueur, such as Cointreau, into each chocolate mixture.

White choc mousse cups

Irresistible, thin and crispy tartlets, full of light white chocolate mousse. Serve with fresh fruit compote and curls of white chocolate.

Serves 6
Preparation time:
 40 minutes + 2 hours
 chilling + cooling
Cooking time:
 9–10 minutes

125 g (4½ oz) chilled **filo pastry**
25 g (1 oz) **butter**, melted

Mousse
50 g (1¾ oz) good quality **white chocolate**, broken into pieces
150 ml (5 fl oz) **double cream**
1 **gelatine sheet**, cut into pieces
1 large **egg**, separated
25 g (1 oz) **caster sugar**

To serve
blueberry and nectarine compote
white chocolate curls

Preheat the oven to 190°C/375°F/Gas Mark 5. Invert six individual, loose bottomed flan tins or dariole moulds (without the bases) on a baking sheet. Cut each sheet of filo pastry into four rectangles and keep them covered with a clean tea towel while working.

Using half the pastry, drape the rectangles in layers over the tins, brushing very lightly with melted butter between each one. Repeat with the remaining pastry to make six tartlets. Trim the top edges. Bake for 9–10 minutes until pale golden and crisp. Cool for 10 minutes, then ease the pastry cases off the tins. Set aside.

Put the chocolate and 25 ml (1 fl oz) of the cream in a heatproof bowl and melt slowly over a pan of gently simmering water.

Put the gelatine into 2 tablespoons of water and leave to soak for 10 minutes. Pour into the warm chocolate cream and stir gently until dissolved and smooth. Stir in the egg yolk.

Whisk the egg white until it forms soft peaks, then gradually whisk in the sugar until stiff. Whisk the remaining cream until it just begins to hold its shape.

Using a metal spoon, fold the meringue and whipped cream into the chocolate and spoon immediately into the cases. Chill to set for about 2 hours, then serve with the blueberry and nectarine compote and white chocolate curls.

Tip The filled tartlets can be made and frozen ahead of time. Thaw in the fridge for 15 minutes before serving.

Chocolate & Muscatel flan

Serve this elegant flan at Christmas with a glass of raisiny liqueur muscat wine to accompany. Use a 375 g pack of ready-made chilled shortcrust pastry if you wish.

Serves 6–8
Preparation time:
  40 minutes + soaking + at least 4½ hours chilling + setting
Cooking time:
  25 minutes

100 g (3½ oz) **Muscatel raisins**
a pinch of **mixed spice**
50 ml (2 fl oz) **dessert wine** or **sherry**
1 quantity **Rich shortcrust pastry** (see page 8)

Chocolate mousse
150 g (5½ oz) **plain chocolate**, broken into pieces
100 g (3½ oz) **unsalted butter**
3 small **eggs**, separated
50 g (1¾ oz) **caster sugar**

Icing
50 g (1¾ oz) **plain chocolate**, broken into pieces
15 g (½ oz) **unsalted butter**
3 tablespoons **double cream**

Put the raisins in a bowl and add the mixed spice and dessert wine or sherry. Leave to soak overnight.

Put a baking sheet in the oven and preheat to 200°C/400°F/Gas Mark 6. Roll out the pastry on a lightly floured surface to about 3 mm (⅛ inch) thick, then use it to line a 23 cm (9 inch) loose-based, fluted flan tin, about 2.5 cm (1 inch) deep. Prick the base with a fork and pop in the freezer for 30 minutes.

Line the pastry case with a sheet of foil, pressing it gently into the curves of the tin and folding it down carefully over the outside. Fill with baking beans and bake on the baking sheet for 15 minutes.

Remove the foil and beans, then bake for a further 10 minutes or until the pastry is firm, pale golden brown and cooked through. If necessary, use a little beaten egg to brush over any cracks and return to the oven for 2–3 minutes to seal.

For the mousse, place the chocolate in a heatproof bowl over a pan of gently simmering water. Stir until melted, remove from the heat and add the butter. Stir until melted and smooth. Beat the egg yolks into the chocolate.

Whisk the egg whites to a soft peak, whisk in the caster sugar and continue to whisk until firm. Fold the egg whites into the chocolate mixture with a metal spoon.

Spoon the soaked muscatels evenly over the base of the prepared pastry case. Pour over the chocolate mousse and spread with a spatula to smooth. Chill for at least 4 hours or overnight.

To prepare the icing, melt the chocolate as above. Add the butter and stir until melted. Stir in the cream and mix thoroughly. Pour the icing on to the chilled mousse, spreading evenly to the edges. Allow to set, then decorate in a crisscross pattern with a hot knife.

Tips The finished flan can be frozen. To use, thaw overnight at cool room temperature.

For a glossy finish to the tart, wave a kitchen blow torch gently over the icing before serving.

Tiramisu tart

A glorious, rich creamy tart based on the famous Italian pudding. It is perfect as a dessert or for a special afternoon tea.

Serves 8–10
Preparation time:
20 minutes +
1½ hours chilling
Cooking time:
30–35 minutes

225 g (8 oz) chilled **'all
    butter' puff pastry**
25 g (1 oz) **butter**, melted
1 **egg yolk**
2 teaspoons **caster sugar**
1 teaspoon **vanilla extract**
250 g tub **mascarpone**
100 ml (3½ fl oz) **double
    cream**
1 teaspoon **icing sugar**
2 tablespoons strong cold
    black **coffee**
2 tablespoons **Tia Maria** or
    other **coffee-flavoured
    liqueur**
3 **Savoiardi** or **sponge
    fingers**, broken or
    chopped into small pieces
cocoa powder and **icing
    sugar**, for dusting

Put a baking sheet in the oven and preheat to 220°C/425°F/Gas Mark 7.

Roll out the pastry thinly on a lightly floured surface, then use to line a 34 x 11.5 cm (13½ x 4½ inch) loose-based tranche tin. Prick the base with a fork and pop in the freezer for 30 minutes.

Line the pastry case with a sheet of foil, pressing it gently into the curves of the tin and folding it down over the outside. Fill with baking beans and bake on the baking sheet for 15 minutes.

Remove the foil and beans, then bake for a further 15–20 minutes or until the pastry is golden and cooked through. Cover with foil if necessary until the pastry case is crisp.

Beat the egg yolk with the caster sugar until pale and thick, then add the vanilla extract and mascarpone and whisk until evenly mixed. Lightly whip the cream with the icing sugar and fold gently into the mascarpone mixture. Spoon half the mixture carefully over the base of the pastry case.

Mix together the coffee and Tia Maria. Briefly submerge the biscuit pieces, a few at a time, in the coffee liquid and arrange evenly on top of the mascarpone.

Spoon the remaining mascarpone mixture over the biscuits and chill for 1 hour. Dust the top of the filling with stripes of cocoa powder and the pastry with icing sugar. Serve cut into fingers.

Tip To make the cocoa stripes, cut a strip of greaseproof paper and lay it diagonally over the filling. Dust with cocoa powder, moving the paper as you move up the tart.

Berry & elderflower tart

Sharp, tender gooseberries with a hint of elderflower, all in a light pastry. Delicious! Use a 375 g pack of ready-made chilled shortcrust pastry if you wish.

Serves 8
Preparation time:
30 minutes +
30 minutes chilling +
overnight soaking +
1 hour cooling
Cooking time:
55–60 minutes

450 g (1 lb) ripe
  gooseberries, topped and
  tailed
50 ml (2 fl oz) **elderflower
  cordial**
1 large quantity **Rich
  shortcrust pastry** (see Tip,
  page 8)
3 **eggs**
100 g (3½ oz) **caster sugar**
300 ml (10 fl oz) **double
  cream**
1 teaspoon **vanilla extract**

Prick the gooseberries with a cocktail stick and drop into a bowl. Pour over the cordial and leave to soak overnight.

Put a baking sheet in the oven and preheat to 200°C/400°F/Gas Mark 6.

Roll out the pastry on a lightly floured surface to about 3 mm (⅛ inch) thick, then use it to line a 23 cm (9 inch) loose-based, fluted flan tin, about 4.5–5 cm (1¾–2 inches) deep. Prick the base with a fork and pop in the freezer for 30 minutes.

Line the pastry case with a sheet of foil, pressing it gently into the curves of the tin and folding it down carefully over the outside. Fill with baking beans and bake on the baking sheet for 15 minutes.

Remove the foil and beans, then bake for a further 5–10 minutes or until the pastry is firm and pale golden brown around the edges. If necessary, use a little beaten egg to brush over any cracks and return to the oven for 2–3 minutes to seal. Reduce the oven temperature to 180°C/350°F/Gas Mark 4.

Mix together the eggs, sugar, cream and vanilla extract in a jug.

Drain the gooseberries and spoon them into the prepared pastry case. Pour over the egg mixture. Bake for 35 minutes until the centre is just firm. Leave to cool for 1 hour before serving.

Tip To glaze the tart, warm 3 tablespoons of apricot conserve with 1 tablespoon of boiling water. Brush evenly over the cold tart to cover completely.

Lemon fudge flan

This tart filling has the texture of thick buttery fudge but with a delicious sharp citrus flavour. Perfect with fresh raspberries.

Serves 8
Preparation time:
  20 minutes +
  overnight chilling +
  1 hour resting +
  cooling
Cooking time: 1 hour
  50 minutes–2 hours
  10 minutes

75 g (2¾ oz) **plain white flour**
2 teaspoons **icing sugar**, plus extra for dusting
150 g (5½ oz) **butter**
grated zest and juice of 2 small **lemons** (about 100 ml/3½ fl oz)
5 **eggs**
150 g (5½ oz) **caster sugar**
400 g (14 oz) fresh **raspberries**, to decorate

Preheat the oven to 170°C/325°F/Gas Mark 3.

Blend together the flour, icing sugar and 50 g (1¾ oz) of the butter in a food processor until the mixture resembles breadcrumbs. Spoon into a 23 cm (9 inch) round, 2.5 cm (1 inch) deep ceramic flan dish. Using your fingertips, press into the base and up the sides. Bake for about 35–40 minutes or until golden. Reduce the oven temperature to 130°C/250°F/Gas Mark ½.

Melt the remaining butter and put in a food processor with the lemon zest and juice, eggs and sugar. Blend until smooth, then pour into the warm tart case (the case must be warm when the filling is poured in or the pastry crumbs will rise to the surface).

Bake the tart for 1¼–1½ hours or until just set. Leave to cool then cover and chill overnight.

To serve, remove from the fridge and leave at room temperature for 1 hour. Dust heavily with icing sugar, caramelise with a cook's blowtorch and scatter with fresh raspberries.

Pineapple coconut tartlets

Coconut pastry is sweet and crisp and perfect for a tropical filling. Use a 375 g pack of ready-made chilled dessert pastry if you wish.

Serves 12
Preparation time:
  50 minutes +
  30 minutes chilling +
  cooling
Cooking time:
  15–20 minutes

1 quantity **Coconut pastry**
  (see page 12)

Coconut cream
25 g (1 oz) **palm sugar**
1 **egg yolk**
1 teaspoon **plain flour**
1 teaspoon **cornflour**
75 ml (3 fl oz) **coconut milk**
25 ml (1 fl oz) extra thick
  double cream

Topping
½ **papaya**, peeled, stoned
  and thinly sliced
¼ small **pineapple**, peeled
  and thinly sliced
4–5 **kiwi berries**, halved, or
  1 small **kiwi fruit**, peeled
  and thinly sliced
toasted **coconut shreds**

Put a baking sheet in the oven and preheat to 200°C/400°F/Gas Mark 6. Roll out the pastry on a lightly floured surface to about 3 mm (⅛ inch) thick, then use it to line 12-hole shallow bun tin. Prick the bases with a fork and pop in the freezer for 30 minutes.

Line each pastry case with a small sheet of foil, pressing it gently into the curves of the tin and folding it down carefully over the outside. Fill the cases with baking beans and bake on the baking sheet for 10 minutes.

Remove the foil and beans, then bake for a further 5–7 minutes or until the pastry is firm and golden brown. If necessary, use a little beaten egg to brush over any cracks and return to the oven for 2–3 minutes to seal.

To make the coconut cream, put the palm sugar in a saucepan and melt slowly over a gently heat. Increase the heat and allow the sugar to caramelise. This will take just a few seconds so don't take your eyes off it! Add 2 tablespoons of water and stir over the heat until smooth. Beat together the egg yolk, flour and cornflour and stir in the caramel mixture.

Bring the coconut milk to the boil and pour into the caramel mixture, stirring all the time. Return to the saucepan and bring to the boil, stirring, until it forms a thick custard. Pour into a bowl, cover with damp greaseproof paper and leave to cool. Once cold, fold in the double cream.

When ready to serve, fill the tartlets with the coconut cream, top with the prepared fruit and decorate with toasted coconut. Serve within 1 hour.

Tip The coconut cream and the fruit topping can be served in individual filo tartlet cases. To make these, see Rhubarb crumbly tarts, page 58.

Fig & fennel tart

The combination of sweet dried figs and tart apples is simply delicious with fragrant fennel.

Serves 8
Preparation time:
  25 minutes +
  overnight soaking +
  cooling
Cooking time:
  20 minutes

1 quantity **Rich shortcrust pastry** (see page 8)

Filling
12 small **dried figs**
150 ml (5 fl oz) **apple juice**
2 tablespoons **demerara sugar**
a large pinch of **fennel seeds**
4 small, tart **eating apples**, peeled, cored and sliced
2 tablespoons **lemon juice**
1 **egg yolk**
2 teaspoons **milk**
caster sugar, for sprinkling

Soak the figs in the apple juice overnight.

The next day, put the demerara sugar and fennel seeds in a pestle and mortar and crush to a rough powder. Stir the fennel mixture into the apples and stir in the lemon juice.

Preheat the oven to 200°C/400°F/Gas Mark 6. Thinly roll out the pastry on a lightly floured surface to about 35.5 cm (14 inches) in diameter and place in a 23 cm (9 inch) loose-based flan tin. Press over the base and into the sides, but do not trim away the edges.

Spoon the apple mixture into the tin. Drain the figs of any excess liquid and arrange on top. Fold the excess pastry up and over the figs to cover. Mix the egg yolk with the milk and use to glaze the pastry. Sprinkle generously with caster sugar.

Bake for about 20 minutes or until well browned. Cool slightly before serving.

Sweet ricotta tart

Serve in slim wedges with coffee or top with fruit compotes to serve as pudding.
Use 1½ x 375 g packs of ready-made chilled dessert pastry if you wish.

Serves 8–10
Preparation time:
  20 minutes +
  30 minutes chilling
Cooking time:
  60–65 minutes

1 large quantity **Sweet flan pastry** (see Tip, page 9)
200 g (7 oz) **full fat soft cheese**
200 g (7 oz) **ricotta cheese**
225 ml (8 fl oz) **double cream**
3 large **eggs**
40 g (1½ oz) **caster sugar**
1 level tablespoon **plain white flour**
1 tablespoon **vanilla extract**

Put a baking sheet in the oven and preheat to 200°C/400°F/Gas Mark 6. Roll out the pastry on a lightly floured surface to about 3 mm (⅛ inch) thick, then use it to line a 23 cm (9 inch) loose-based, fluted flan tin, about 4.5–5 cm (1¾–2 inches) deep. Prick the base with a fork and pop in the freezer for 30 minutes.

Line the pastry case with a sheet of foil, pressing it gently into the curves of the tin and folding it down carefully over the outside. Fill with baking beans and bake on the baking sheet for 15 minutes.

Remove the foil and beans, then bake for a further 5–10 minutes or until the pastry is firm and pale golden brown around the edges. Reduce the oven temperature to 180°C/350°F/Gas Mark 4.

Meanwhile, beat together the cheeses, cream and eggs. Stir in the sugar with the flour and vanilla extract. Pour the mixture into the pastry case and bake for a further 40 minutes or until just set.

Variation Spread the pastry base with a good quality conserve before pouring on the cheese mixture.

Iced chestnut parfaits

The very lightest of whipped chestnut meringue blended and then frozen with Irish mist. A great alternative pudding for Christmas.

Serves 6
Preparation time:
  20 minutes + at least
  4 hours freezing +
  30 minutes chilling +
  cooling
Cooking time:
  5 minutes

125 g (4½ oz) chilled **filo pastry**
25 g (1 oz) **butter**, melted
3 tablespoons **sweet chestnut purée**
4 **egg whites**
125 g (4½ oz) **icing sugar**, sieved
150 ml (5 fl oz) **double cream**, lightly whipped
2 tablespoons **whisky-based cream liqueur**, such as Baileys, plus extra to serve

To decorate
caramelised chestnuts (see Tips)
caster sugar

Put a baking sheet in the oven and preheat to 190°C/375°F/Gas Mark 5. Cut the filo pastry into 12 x 15 cm (6 inch) squares. Brush a filo square with a little of the melted butter and press down firmly into one hole of a 6-hole deep muffin tin. Lay two more pieces of buttered filo pastry on top and press down. Repeat with all the other muffin holes. Chill for 30 minutes then carefully trim the edges to neaten. Meanwhile, stamp out six 7.5 cm (3 inch) rounds from the remaining filo pastry and place on a baking sheet.

Bake the cases for 5 minutes or until the pastry is golden and crisp. Bake the pastry rounds for 2–3 minutes until golden. Cool for 5 minutes before easing the cases out of the tins on to the baking sheet.

Whisk the egg whites until stiff, then gradually whisk in the icing sugar. Fold in the chestnut purée, cream and liqueur. Spoon into the filo cases and freeze for at least 4 hours.

Put the tartlets on serving plates, top with a caramelised chestnut and a crisp round of filo pastry and dust with caster sugar. Serve immediately.

Tips Because of the alcohol in the meringue, the mixture does not freeze solidly, so the tartlets can be served from frozen.

To caramelise chestnuts, melt 100 g (3½ oz) of caster sugar over a low heat. When the sugar turns a deep caramel colour, stir in 3 tablespoons of water. It will splutter! Stir until smooth. Add 125 g (4½ oz) of whole, cooked, peeled chestnuts, stir to coat in the caramel and leave to cool.

Crème brûlée tart

This is the perfect pudding for preparing ahead with sweet custard offset by refreshing clementines. Use 1½ x 375 g packs of ready-made chilled dessert pastry if you wish.

Serves 8–10
Preparation time:
  30 minutes +
  overnight chilling
Cooking time:
  20–25 minutes

1 large quantity **Sweet flan pastry** (see Tip, page 9)
6 **egg yolks**
150 g (5½ oz) **caster sugar**
1 teaspoon **cornflour**
900 ml (1½ pints) **double cream**
6 small **clementines**, peeled and thinly sliced, peel reserved

Put a baking sheet in the oven and preheat to 200°C/400°F/Gas Mark 6. Roll out the pastry on a lightly floured surface to about 3 mm (⅛ inch) thick, then use it to line a 23 cm (9 inch) loose-based, fluted flan tin, about 4.5–5 cm (1¾–2 inches) deep. Prick the base with a fork and pop in the freezer for 30 minutes.

Line the pastry case with a sheet of foil, pressing it gently into the curves of the tin and folding it down carefully over the outside. Fill with baking beans and bake on the baking sheet for 15 minutes.

Remove the foil and beans, then bake for a further 5–10 minutes or until the pastry is firm and pale golden brown around the edges. If necessary, use a little beaten egg to brush over any cracks and return to the oven for 2–3 minutes to seal.

Beat together the egg yolks, 75 g (2¾ oz) of sugar and the cornflour. Put the cream in a saucepan with a handful of clementine peel and bring up to the boil. Strain over the egg mixture, stirring all the time. Return the mixture to the saucepan and stir over a gentle heat for 10 minutes. Bring to a simmer, without boiling, and pour into the pastry case. Chill overnight, uncovered, to set.

Preheat the grill to hot. Sprinkle a foil-lined baking sheet with the remaining caster sugar, put under the grill and heat for 4–5 minutes until the sugar caramelises. Immediately tilt the baking sheet from side to side so that the caramel covers the foil in a thin layer. Leave to set then break into shards.

Arrange the clementine slices around the outside edge of the tart and sprinkle the sugar 'glass' in the centre.

Variation Stir 50 g (1¾ oz) of finely chopped stem ginger into the hot custard before baking.

Shortbread praline tartlets

This shortbread biscuit dough can be pressed into any size bun or muffin tin to make a sweet, crisp pastry case. Ideal for parties.

Makes 24
Preparation time:
  20 minutes
Cooking time:
  15–20 minutes

50 g (1¾ oz) **unsalted butter**, softened
50 g (1¾ oz) **caster sugar**
1 **egg**, beaten
125 g (4½ oz) **plain flour**
50 g (1¾ oz) **ground almonds**
300 ml (10 fl oz) **double cream**
2 teaspoons **crème de peche/peach liqueur**, (optional)
almond praline (see Tips), to serve

Preheat the oven to 180°C/350°F/Gas Mark 4.

In a bowl, beat together the butter and sugar for a good 5 minutes until pale and fluffy. Gradually beat in the egg, then stir in the flour and almonds to form a rough dough.

Turn out on to a lightly floured surface and bring the mixture together to a soft dough. Divide into 24 equal pieces and roll into balls. Press into flat discs with your fingers and use to line two 12-hole mini muffin tins. Bake for 15–20 minutes until golden (keep an eye on them as they will change colour very quickly). Allow to cool.

Lightly whip the cream and fold in the peach liqueur, if using. Fill the cases with the cream and top with almond praline.

Tips To make almond praline, put 50 g (1¾ oz) of caster sugar in a small, heavy-based saucepan. Place over a low heat until the sugar has completely dissolved and turned a pale golden caramel. Stir in 25 g (1 oz) of toasted flaked almonds and turn out on to oiled foil. Leave to harden, then break into chunks.

The unfilled cases will keep in an airtight container for 3–4 days.

You can also make 12 larger cases by baking the same quantity of dough in a 12-hole bun tin. Bake for 15–20 minutes.

Variations Fill with the coconut cream from page 98.

Fill with small scoops of vanilla ice cream and freeze. Serve from frozen topped with chopped nuts or salted caramel (see page 81).

Fill with the vanilla mascarpone cream from page 38.

Warm berry puffs

Make this pudding when summer fruits are cheap and plentiful. You can buy vanilla sugar or make your own (see Tip).

Serves 6
Preparation time:
20 minutes + cooling
Cooking time:
45–50 minutes

225 g (8 oz) chilled **puff pastry**
1 **egg**, beaten
caster sugar, to glaze
rum and raisin ice cream, to serve

Berry compote
175 g (6 oz) fresh **cherries**, stoned
125 g (4½ oz) **blueberries**
50 g (1¾ oz) **vanilla caster sugar** (see Tip)
4 tablespoons **redcurrant jelly**
125 ml (4 fl oz) **red wine**
pared rind of 1 **orange**
400 g (14 oz) **strawberries**, hulled and halved if large
150 g (5½ oz) **raspberries**

Preheat the oven to 180°C/350°F/Gas Mark 4. Place the cherries and blueberries in a large, shallow, ovenproof dish and add the sugar, redcurrant jelly, wine and orange rind. Bake in the preheated oven, uncovered, for 15 minutes. Stir occasionally.

Stir in the strawberries and return the dish to the oven for 10–15 minutes, or until the fruits are tender and the juices begin to run. Remove the dish from the oven and stir in the raspberries. Leave to cool.

Increase the oven temperature to 200°C/400°F/Gas Mark 6. Spoon the fruit into six individual ceramic dishes, ovenproof cups or large ramekin dishes.

Roll the pastry out on a lightly floured surface and stamp out six rounds slightly larger than the top of the dishes being used.

Brush the top of the dishes with beaten egg and press the pastry rounds on top. Brush the pastry with egg and sprinkle generously with caster sugar. Bake for 20 minutes or until puffed and golden.

Split open the hot pastry and drop a scoop of rum and raisin ice cream into the centre of the pies. Serve immediately

Tip To make vanilla sugar, fill a kilner jar or jam jar with caster sugar. Split open a vanilla pod and push it down into the sugar. Seal the jar and leave for at least 1 week. Top up the sugar as you use it.

Valentine hearts

A simple pudding to assemble and serve for a Valentine's dinner. Any leftover custard can be frozen for a later date.

Serves 2
Preparation time:
  20 minutes
Cooking time:
  20–30 minutes

1 tablespoon **Limoncello liqueur**
75 g (2¾ oz) fresh **raspberries** or **blackberries**
75 g (2¾ oz) chilled **puff pastry**
1 teaspoon **raspberry conserve**
50 ml (2 fl oz) good quality, fresh, ready-made **vanilla custard**, plus extra to serve
1 small **egg yolk**
icing sugar, for dusting

Preheat the oven to 200°C/400°F/Gas Mark 6. Stir the Limoncello gently through the raspberries and set aside.

Roll the pastry out on a lightly floured surface to 3 mm (⅛ inch) thick. Stamp or cut out two large hearts. Score a 1.25 cm (½ inch) border inside each heart. Prick inside the border with a fork, arrange on a baking sheet and bake for 10–15 minutes or until pale golden and risen. Remove from the oven and turn the heat down to 180°C/350°F/Gas Mark 4.

Press down the centre of each pastry heart to form a hollow. Spread the raspberry conserve over the base of each one.

Beat the custard with the egg yolk and divide between the cases. Dot with the raspberries and bake in the oven for 10–15 minutes or until just set. Cool slightly before serving with a little extra custard and dusted with icing sugar.

Index